DRAWN FROM THE PLAINS

Life in the Wilds of Namibia and Moçambique

Lynne Tinley

Illustrations by the author

authorHOUSE®

AuthorHouse™
1663 Liberty Drive, Suite 200
Bloomington, IN 47403
www.authorhouse.com
Phone: 1-800-839-8640

First published by AuthorHouse 1/31/2008
First edition published by William Collins Sons & Co Ltd, London, 1979.

ISBN: 978-1-4343-3948-5 (sc)
ISBN: 978-1-4343-3949-2 (hc)

Printed in the United States of America
Bloomington, Indiana

This book is printed on acid-free paper.

Lynne Tinley and her husband Ken, who is one of the leading ecologists in Africa, have devoted many years to a race against time. On the Etosha Pan, in the isolated and spectacular wildernesses of Namibia, and later on the other side of the continent at Gorongosa in Moçambique, they set out to gather information which was urgently needed if the natural ecological balances of these and other African parks and reserves were to be preserved.

Living in the wilderness they discovered a wealth of wonders. Sketching this far-off world of risk and hardship in words and pictures Lynne conveys images of great beauty, controversial biology, anthropology and veld humour. Moreover she provides a vivid and entertaining account of how to raise a boy and girl in the bush. Together the family survives terrorist raids, charging hippo, elephant and lion, rabid dog bites, baboon spiders, gaboon vipers, acid-shooting beetles, alcoholic snails, dangling camel membranes, and the Fat Mouse. They eat elephant trunk Portuguese-style and termites cooked by bushmen.

From Otjovasandu—"The place where the elephants come through"—to the wind-swept desert pan at Okaukuejo, to the Cheringoma Plateau, through burning midday mirage and freezing lion-roaring, baboon-sobbing nights, with great sensitivity and fatalism, and an eye for the peculiarities of those who live to survive in the outer reaches, Lynne Tinley records an incredible, fast-moving period of human and animal history.

Peter Beard
Nahoon River Mouth
South Africa 1979

To Ken
for widening the horizons in my life

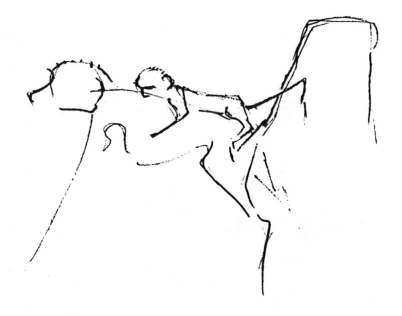

CONTENTS

MAPS

(by Ken Tinley)

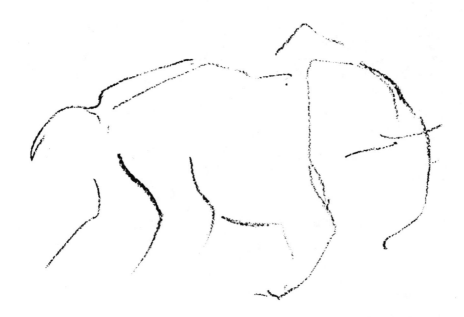

INTRODUCTION

As an eleven-year-old tomboy I had a gently rocking niche high in a willow tree in the garden where I used to sit and sway with every breeze: my back, bare feet and legs propped against the branches. The live musty smell of the bark bit into my nostrils, and in early spring the sticky flower-catkins shook their delicate scent around me. Far away over the rooftops the sun would set deeply crimson behind the slow smoke pall of Johannesburg, the rough square mine dumps heaving up blackly before it. In the stillness of dusk, drums would begin to beat from the mine compounds not far away. The throbbing pulse carried me in my adolescent imagination far into the very depth of Africa. That violent orb of the sun was Africa; the compulsive primitive resonance of the drums was Africa; I was Africa. The houses, roads and neat square gardens of the mine property around me were foreign: a piece of Europe lifted up and set mundanely on the highveld. Beyond the opaque smog was Africa and my being pulled towards it, yearning to be part of it and its raw red earth.

While that immature, thin-limbed girl was aching to communicate with the land in which she was born but of which she still knew so little, a blond eighteen-year-old boy was beginning life as a game ranger in remote reaches of northern Zululand. Born on a farm in the midlands of that country, Ken had grown up among the native people, with the various inhabitants of the tangled forest – monkey, antelope and robin – at his front door. Much of his boyhood was spent with Zulu children – *umfaans* – as his playmates, and with them he explored the hills and forests and hunted cane rat with sharpened stick spears.

Six years of living and working as a ranger in the wilderness of the Tongaland Plain, absorbing and recording every aspect of the natural environment from the lie of the landscape and the cut of the rivers to the vegetation, animal life, and climatic cycles, matured Ken into a proficient and perceptive ecologist. But he still needed a university degree to give credence and polish to his work. Resigning his post with the Parks, he enrolled in 1961 at the University of Pietermaritzburg in Natal for a Bachelor of Science degree.

By some quirk of Fate I, now seventeen, enrolled at the same University to study the same subjects – zoology, botany and geology. Surprisingly considerate of our studies and future careers, Fate did not allow Ken and me to get to know each other until three years later. Then she allowed destiny to take its course and we became friendly just three weeks before our final exams. Nevertheless we both passed!

Three months later we married. We were newly qualified and eager for fresh horizons. Africa lay before us, passive and inscrutable, open to us only if we dared, as so many do not, to break the ties of security and materialism that safe city jobs provide and go out to explore.

In October of 1965 Ken took a post as assistant biologist in the Etosha National Park, South West Africa (now known as Namibia). We were based at Etosha for three years, during which we travelled extensively through the territory of the South West. In 1968 we moved from the west to the east of southern Africa and lived and worked in Gorongosa National Park in the magnificently wild interior of Moçambique.

Over the years two children were born to us: Allan, whilst we were in Etosha, and Michelle in Gorongosa. The babies went everywhere with us, sleeping under mosquito nets at night, accepting the Land-Rover as home at times and swarms of flies and prickly heat as a natural part of living. Allan's toys were frogs, insects and other animals; and he did not have a pair of bought shoes until he was five years old. A miniature pair of the rough sandals that Africans make from car tyre rubber covered his small feet in thorny country. Both children learnt Portuguese from black playmates in Moçambique as soon as they started to speak and like us they absorbed the warm human atmosphere that existed between races in that lovely country.

Now, after almost ten years of living in wild and remote places, we have returned temporarily to a city, Pretoria, while Ken analyses and compiles his Gorongosa data for a doctoral thesis. The natural world haunts us while we are here, calling almost as strongly as it did to that child in the willow tree – but the bond is deeper, more sure. We will go back, we know we will, because it is only there that we are truly alive. Only out on the plains or hills with the sun scorching our backs and rivulets of sweat streaking our faces: where daily survival depends on individual senses and versatility; where one is acutely aware of being alive, and an integral part of the natural environment.

The completion of this book is due in part to my good friend Derryn Hurry, who gave me very necessary encouragement to go on with it. Ian Player, conservationist, author and game-ranging mentor and friend from Ken's Tongaland years, kindly read through the manuscript and added his advice.

The ecological observations in my book, unless otherwise stated, are all Ken's. They are so much a part of our life and thought that they have often slipped in unconsciously. The drawings and paintings that I have included do not necessarily illustrate the text: they are mostly taken from my field sketch books and are comments in their own right on animals, people or places at the time I knew them.

Lynne Tinley 1979

Post Script

For the second edition of this book I would like to thank the Carr Foundation who took the project on so willingly and competently, and our dear friend, scientist and colleague, Antoni Milewski for his editing help. The Royalties from the sale of this book will be donated to the school at Vinho on the border of Gorongosa National Park, Moçambique.

Ken and I and our three grown children are now living in Western Australia. The arid outback of this vast part of the island continent reminds us of Namibia and Ken has worked with pastoralists toward managing their sheep and cattle stations ecologically. I am putting all of my creative energies into paintings of the Australian landscape and its wildlife. My work can be seen on www.lynnnetinley.com.

Lynne Tinley 2007

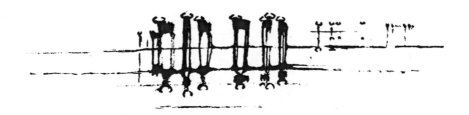

Part One
NAMIBIA

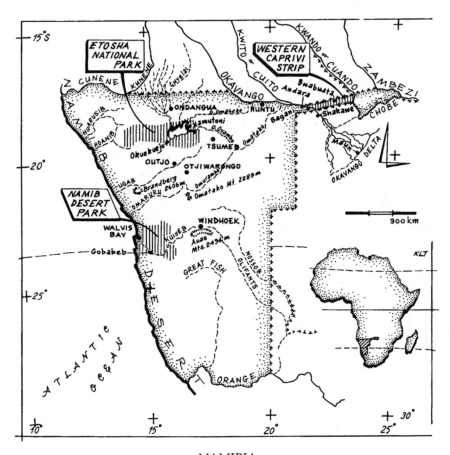

NAMIBIA

I

Etosha

The diesel train engine, pulling effortlessly ahead, now and again let out its probing melancholy call. In two days it had transported Ken and me and our scant luggage (much of it in cardboard boxes) from the east coast to the west coast of southern Africa; from the mountains and an unseasonal snowfall of Natal in the east to the sun-baked semi-deserts, rigid grey horizons and strange rocky *inselbergs* of the north western Cape and Namibia. That evening the sun set purple on the last voluptuous rain clouds we were to see for months as we passed ever deeper into the arid lands. The sky crimsoned and darkened as mist curtains of rain fell remotely and delicately on the wide horizon. The sky seemed to take up so much more space here in these flat landscapes and imparted an atmosphere of purity and freedom.

We were to see a lot more sky and flat land as we travelled on, westward and then north towards the Etosha National Park and a new life. On awakening the next morning our eyes met a linear horizon that appeared to have been drawn with a ruler. Boulders, grey and brown, large and small, lay scattered on the uninterrupted plain and low clay-coloured bushes spiked up between them. In the first sunlight we saw an orange-coloured steenbuck; and further on as the landscape became even more barren a pair of camels, as grey as the dust, surveyed their piece of land with camelesque superiority. Their arrogance seemed fitting, as though they were indeed the only animals fit to survive and rule in this naked country.

Once arrived in Windhoek, the capital of Namibia, we changed to a train bound for the mines of Tsumeb. Through that night and the next day we travelled across thornveld and grassland to Otjiwarongo. Another change here and then on to Outjo. These were names to be wondered at,

1

rolled on the tongue; no longer standing for pictures in our imagination but for reality and a new way of life. They were strange places to us and yet they were pervaded by an atmosphere typical of our southern half of Africa. The details were new but basically these towns and the railway stations that shot by were familiar to us by their very brilliant sunshine, by their spiky thorn bushes, and by the dark faces of the local people.

At Outjo, on the fifth day of our journey, we finally disembarked. The long platform and new brick building of the station looked as conspicuously out of place in the emptiness of the surrounding landscape as an ink blot on a clean white page. Mr. Blom, a motor mechanic from the park, had been sent from Etosha to meet us, and after packing our luggage into his truck we drove through the dusty streets of the small town which looked disillusioned and lifeless in the glaring sunlight of midday.

Heading north we sped along a limestone gravel road which was painfully bright to the eyes, the heat reflecting off its surface with the same intensity as from the sun. The road was wide and in good condition; we travelled fast, almost too fast to take in all that was new to us. The first mopane tree that I had ever seen appeared at the side of the road followed by many more, and soon the whole country was dominated by these grey-barked trees with their lime-green butterfly leaves. The mopane is well known in the drier areas of south-central Africa, and here in Namibia the Outjo district is its southernmost limit. Between the mopane stood bushy *deurmekaar* trees, hung with clusters of brilliant red pods. The Afrikaans people call this the 'mixed up tree', as its branches and twigs are very spiky and intertwined. Hornbills flapped across the road in their crazy swooping flight and flocks of shot-silk glossy starlings flashed up. Thin cattle walked the overgrazed farmlands and here and there a sharp-topped *koppie* broke the monotony of the flatness.

At last we saw far ahead of us a huge stone gateway with a thatched roof: the entrance to Etosha National Park, which was to be our home for the next three years. At that time Etosha was the largest game reserve in the world. It extended across most of north-western Namibia, and included all of the Kaokoveld mountains and the Skeleton Coast – a wide wild country of stunning contrasts and fierce seasonal changes.

Once we were through the gate, Blom slowed his breakneck speed and we began to take in our new environment. Our first impression was that there was not a blade of grass in sight. It was October, the height of the dry season. The landscape was utterly bleached and dry; white outcrops of calcrete rock showed like bones through the grey earth, and the remnants of last season's grasses remained only under fallen branches or trees where the grazing herds and their trampling feet could not reach them.

Towering necks of giraffe jutted above the monotone of leafless thornbush; their faces with long upper lips and curious eyes turned towards us. Springbok crossed the road, and in the distance gemsbok antelope stood, pale forms against pale, bare ground. But despite the barrenness none of these animals was in poor condition: they looked fat and shiny. About half a kilometre away on the flats a herd of white elephant was feeding amongst pink and purple salt bushes. Their hides were whitened by the ubiquitous lime dust that seemed to cover everything in Etosha.

Blom took us to the Okaukuejo Rest Camp, where we were to live. Etosha Park has three camps: Okaukuejo, Halali, and Namutoni. The main camp, Okaukuejo, used to be a police outpost in the days when Germany colonized Namibia, but now it is a village for the park's staff.

Here we saw for the first time the indigenous people of the Etosha area, the Heiqum. They are short and yellow-skinned, with rather flat Asiatic looking faces of the hottentot people. Although they are a hottentot race they are known locally as Heiqum 'bushmen' because of their hunter-gatherer way of life, which is more characteristic of bushmen. They speak a dialect of the Nama hottentot tongue – a soft-sounding language with many subtle clicks. Okaukuejo is a Heiqum word and is reputedly an expletive referring to someone's grandmother's posterior.

Heiqum people once used to live and hunt over the whole of Etosha, but in the last twenty years or so they have been forced to give up their traditional way of life in this area as no hunting is allowed in the park. The Etosha Heiqum now live in a camp at Okaukuejo and are employed as labourers, drivers, game guards, and trackers.

On our arrival a Heiqum nicknamed Simon came to work for Ken as a tracker. (As with the rest of his people his own name with the inevitable clicks in it was too complicated for the white man to pronounce!) Simon had grown up in the Okaukuejo camp and he worked very happily with Ken, showing him around the veld, supplying information concerning plants and animals as well as their local names and uses. He showed us which plants were good to eat, a bush from which the Heiqum make tea, even a grey-green bush whose crushed leaves can be used as soap. However we found that Simon was only happy as long as he remained in Etosha. We once took him on a trip with us to the Caprivi Strip; and after a few weeks Simon seemed to wilt. His ochre face grew longer by the day, his usually alert actions dull and listless. We returned to Etosha for an interlude and found as we were about to go back to the Caprivi that Simon could not go with us. Unwilling or unable to explain to Ken why he did not want to leave Etosha he had cut a finger to the bone with an axe and was unfit to travel. Puzzled at first by his behaviour we concluded that poor Simon must have been so homesick away from his people that he could not bear to be removed from the group again and was prepared to do himself bodily harm to prevent it.

This incident illustrated to us the importance of the group, or family, to the hunter-gatherer people. Their social structure has evolved around the importance of, and co-operation within, the group rather than independent evolution of the individual. Simon was literally half alive away from his group; he lost his identity and his reason for living. No amount of persuasion could take him away again.

2

Life at Okaukuejo

Our first night at Okaukuejo was spent in a tourist hut beside a waterhole where elephant, zebra, and talkative flocks of sand grouse drink each evening. The little furniture that we possessed had not yet arrived by rail and truck from Natal so a furnished hut was made available to us. Pieter Stark, then ranger in charge of Etosha, an individualistic and tough German with the mien of a Prussian officer, entertained us to dinner at his home with Elke, his lovely auburn-haired wife, and their four small sons.

At Okaukuejo at ten o'clock each night the diesel electric light engine is turned off and the camp at once becomes as black as the surrounding bush. At ten thirty on this particular evening, Pieter walked part of the way with us towards the hut where we were to sleep. Lion had been calling from the nearby waterhole. We knew that there was no fence around the camp at this point, only a low wall that would be no obstacle to large animals. The rough-haired bush mongrel at our host's heel was restless and barked sporadically. Casually Pieter remarked that she only barked when lion were near. The night was close and without a glimmer of light: even the stars seemed shrouded. We had no torch and Pieter did not offer to lend us one. He said goodnight and disappeared with his dog into the darkness. Ken and I walked slowly and reluctantly on in the general direction of our hut, straight towards the lions' roars.

We could not see one metre ahead of us and would have bumped into a lion before seeing him. I had to trust in our luck and Ken's navigation. Either one or the other stood us in good stead: a few minutes later we were safely ensconced behind the wooden door of the hut, listening with vast relief to the roars that continued seemingly a few paces away.

Owing to the astounding innocence with which I appear to have been afflicted at that stage I did not realize until many years later that Pieter Stark had put us, as newcomers to the park, to the test. We passed, but had we lost and been mauled or eaten I doubt if his conscience would have worried him a jot! Survival of the toughest was still the law in those last pioneering days in that great wilderness area. In the weeks ahead other rangers were to put Ken to further ingenious tests to ascertain his capacity and adaptability for such feats as meat-eating (considered manly in that part of the world) and withstanding nights of black frost whilst camping out with only a thin sleeping bag! His claim to fame in Namibia is still I am quite sure based on the phenomenal amount of *skaapribbetjies* (sheep ribs) and *mieliepap* (thick maize porridge) he could put away at one sitting rather than his scientific ability or ecological acumen!

The living quarters allocated to us at Okaukuejo were a surprise. Arriving in the Etosha wilderness we had not expected to move into a brand new, modern house with three bedrooms and three sleeping porches. But there it was waiting for us as freshly painted, clean and neat as any suburban home. Our few pieces of furniture looked quite silly in the large rooms. After some months we managed to get a double bed and planks and bricks from Outjo with which we could make bookshelves. The Conservation Department had provided a stove, a fridge and a deep freeze unit so that the kitchen at least was well equipped.

From the kitchen window I could see elephant as they strode to the waterhole behind the camp, and thorn trees in the garden spread feathery leaves against the sky. Under the trees the garden was completely bare apart from building rubble, yet it was always busy with birds, some completely new to me such as the brilliant crimson-breasted strike and the dapper and noisy pied babblers. Months later, after the first rains and a crop of weeds, the garden crawled under a surprising and horrifying plague of huge black and purple flightless crickets, which in Afrikaans are called *koringkrieke*. These dreadful animals, jerking about with awkward lunging movements, would eat anything and everything. The sight of them eating each other alive was only surpassed in horror by seeing one eating a damaged part of its own abdomen!

Ken was one of two staff scientists stationed at Okaukuejo. Whilst the majority of the staff was involved in protecting game from poachers, in maintenance of roads, fences and buildings and in the care of tourists,

Ken's work was to look at and study the reserve as a whole. He made himself familiar with the layout of the land and the vegetation—this involved a great deal of travelling as well as studying aerial photographs—and wherever he went he made copious notes and observations.

Using his experience as an ecologist Ken was then able to bring into focus the ever-changing kaleidoscope of interrelations between plant and animal communities, and between them, their habitats and changes in the landscape. These relationships were synthesized to form a picture or template on which to base management programmes. These programmes included fire control, habitat protection or modification, and control of the numbers of various antelope or game species which when overcrowded can damage plant communities to the detriment of either the habitats themselves or other animals. In short Ken helped to maintain a balance of nature within the artificial park boundaries.

As in most national parks and game reserves in Southern Africa the staff of Etosha, mostly Afrikaans- and German-speaking, were clustered together in a small community. Game rangers, tourist officials, mechanics, and scientists lived cheek by jowl in rows of houses with very small suburban-type gardens separating them. The varying backgrounds and interests of the families in these circumstances often create tensions and conflicts, especially as the people are reliant solely upon each other during both working and leisure time. One family would keep a rooster which would drive another family mad; somebody would forget during

the weekly shopping trip to Outjo to bring vital provisions for someone else; somebody's cat would eat somebody's ducklings; a pet wildebeest would trample a neighbour's newly planted garden and be shot in retaliation. There was no escaping from one another and so the petty irritations would fester, often starting long lived feuds.

Our house in Okaukuejo was on the end of a row, so we had only two close neighbours. Pieter and Elke Stark lived opposite us, and Hymie Ebedes, the other scientist, lived next door. Ken was very busy with his work and I with my painting so that we did not have much to do with our neighbours, and when we did we were fortunate in getting on with them extremely well. Hymie Ebedes was short, vague, and untidy: a mild-mannered man with a thatch of black hair and thick-lensed spectacles. A vet employed as biologist in the park, he spent a lot of time on translocation of animals such as black rhino and gemsbok from other more threatened parts of Namibia into Etosha. He later, rather surprisingly we thought, married a vivacious and lovely opera singer, and brought her from two years of study in Milan to the dusty depths of Etosha. Audrey surprised us even more by adapting herself wholeheartedly to her new surroundings and life style.

We enjoyed Hymie and Audrey's friendship immensely but on one occasion I had cause to feel more than a little antagonism towards Hymie; in fact at the time I could well have murdered him! This was no doubt partly due to the fact that I was seven months pregnant and the hot summer weather had begun. I had an appointment to see the doctor in Windhoek (over 400 kilometres away, this was our nearest city), and as Hymie and Audrey were travelling to head office there I thought I would go with them rather than ask Ken to leave his work for a couple of days. So I took a back seat in their Land-Rover station-wagon together with several of the local Heiqum women and children who were going visiting some distance along the road to Outjo. Land-Rover seats are not very comfortable at the best of times, but a back seat when one is heavily pregnant and the roads corrugated is especially uncomfortable. Hymie is a slow and careful driver and by nightfall we were only halfway to Windhoek.

We spent the night at the small town of Otjiwarongo and were up at half past five the next morning in order to reach Windhoek by eleven, when both Audrey and I were due to see our doctors. As it happened Audrey was also a few months pregnant and that morning she was heartily car sick. Once in Windhoek we learned that we must return to Okaukuejo that night as the Land Rover that Hymie was driving was needed for transporting V.I.P.s around the park the next day. Audrey and I saw our doctors and hastened to finish our errands so as to be ready at five o'clock for the long trip home. However the Ebedes' groceries had still to be bought; they were piled into the back of the Rover, together with three new tyres and an upholstered car seat.

Once on the road out of town Hymie remembered he had not picked up my fruit and vegetables as arranged, so back we went. These three cardboard cartons had to travel on the seat next to me as there was no longer any room at the back. By this time Audrey and I were exhausted, hot, and frustrated. Ignoring us both Hymie decided to visit a chicken farm and buy some day-old chicks which he would not otherwise have a chance of getting for several months. To our horror he starting asking prices for fifty chicks when there was hardly enough space in the vehicle for one. Eventually he was persuaded to take only fifteen chicks; but he did add four dozen eggs to our load as well, thus reducing my quota of space on the back seat still further. By now it was half past seven and we had not yet left Windhoek.

After a quick and very necessary supper we at last got on the road. Folded up like a jack-knife on the back seat, fearful that the formidable pile of luggage behind me might come toppling down at the next bad bump or sharp bend, I attempted to sleep. Once or twice we had to stop for Audrey to be sick.

Round about midnight Hymie came across a steenbuck that had been knocked down and killed by an earlier car. Hoping to find parasites on the animal the next morning, Hymie stopped and, horror upon horrors, piled the freshly killed and still bleeding little buck on top of the tottering tower at the back! The smell of blood and entrails from the dead animal made Audrey violently ill again and after several more stops we eventually staggered into Okaukuejo around 2.30 a.m. Exhausted, cramped and cross as I was, I could still forgive Hymie until the next morning when I found that the steenbuck's blood had seeped through a paper carrier on to my library books.

The Starks became our good friends too. Elke was a lovely and talented girl. She played the guitar, sang, and was the only person I've ever met who could hum and whistle at the same. Pieter was fierce and proud, an excellent game ranger who patrolled the reserve regularly either on horseback or by truck, often spending weeks on end out in the veld. Elephant roaming beyond the borders of the park into adjoining farm land was one of his routine problems. He dealt with this in a typical Pieter way. Taking no nonsense from the miscreant elephants he would charge them on horseback cracking a leather whip or *sjambok* over his head. Utterly amazed, the huge animals would turn tail and head back at the double for the safety of the Park!

One bright spring morning Pieter, who handled guns every day of his life, shot himself in the backside. He was taking a .22 pistol out of a cupboard and accidently dropped it. Being loaded it went off and shot him right up the rear end. Elke thought he was going to die: she was almost hysterical. She brought her four boys, all in tears too, across to me, and I had to try to convince them that their father was not dead and was in all probability going to survive. Meanwhile Elke asked the office to radio for an aeroplane from Windhoek. The plane took most of the morning to arrive, during which time I entertained the children as best as I could – a task still foreign to me as I was not yet a mother myself. I tried to prevent the distraught boys from looking out of the windows in case they should see their father being carried off on a stretcher, perhaps unconscious, or bleeding copiously – I had no idea at that stage how extensive his injuries were. Audrey Ebedes came to my aid by loading us all into her car and taking us to Leeubron to look for lions.

Leeubron was a permanent spring some thirty kilometres from Okaukuejo where the Park authorities used at one stage to leave a weekly offering of a zebra carcass for the lion prides. This practice has been discontinued but the spring was still a popular gathering place for lion. On the day we went there were no lion at Leeubron. The area was dry, dusty and bleak, with dun-coloured gemsbok against dun-coloured dust, thorn trees and waterhole. The drive however did us all good, and as we were returning the plane took off over our heads.

We were all vastly relieved to hear that Pieter's bullet wound was not serious, although it could have been had the bullet penetrated just a little bit further and injured the lower nerve centre. Very fortunately it had become lodged at the base of the spine and did not touch the spinal column or the nerves of the legs. Pieter never did have the bullet removed as the operation in itself would have been dangerous. Within a month after the accident he was back on a horse and took first place in an important dressage competition.

In our first year in Etosha Ken and I took riding lessons from Pieter and Elke, who were both accomplished horsemen. Mine came to an end once I fell pregnant. Ken's came to an end soon after he man-handled Pieter's horse when it tried to buck him. According to Pieter, Ken's tall frame leapt from the rearing horse and, standing at its head, he pulled it down to a standstill, roaring, '*Wat moet ek met die donderse ding nou doen?*' (What do I do with the damned thing now?)

One of our favourite friends amongst the staff at Etosha did not live at Okaukuejo but at one of the entrance gates to the park. Uncle Roy Sterley worked at the Ombika gate, where his job was to welcome visitors, take their names and give information. Over seventy when we met him ten years ago, Uncle Roy was stocky and powerfully built, with a cowboy's gait and a poet's heart. He could shoot, ride and throw a knife better than any youngster in the district, possibly better than any man in the south west. The white-haired old man would greet visitors with open arms and a wide lopsided smile over his rugged features. Quoting verses from Omar Khayam he would win the hearts of surprised ladies whilst proudly presenting each with a flower, grown in a little bed near the gate for the purpose! Uncle Roy, at the time we arrived in Etosha, used to live in a shack made of boxwood and hessian. He would sleep there at night with only the sacking between him and the prowling hyaena, and I think that's how he was happiest. We often drank a mug of coffee with him, seated under the cool shade of the hessian. The breeze, leaves and dust of the outside were part of his dwelling: he was part of the veld. Later a house was built for him – a modern brick building with windows, bathroom and all the rest. His wife, Aunty Dolly, moved to Etosha once the house was ready and became the post mistress at Okaukuejo. Uncle Roy's life changed for the better, I'm sure he would be the first to say, but I think he may still have hankered after those earlier days when the wind swept through his shack.

Behind our house there were no other buildings; we looked out on thornveld and, a little way off where a slight rise brought the limestone nearer to the surface, mopane woodland. We became so fond of the mopane tree with its butterfly leaves and its coarse grey bark; and I soon found that it has uses for many different animals as well as for man. Squirrels, owls, hoopoes, barbets and bees live in rot holes that form in the hard red wood. Giant caterpillars that grow to more than six or seven centimetres in length eat the mopane leaves, and are in turn a delicacy to the Heiqum, who toast them to crisp puffs over the coals.

A type of leafhopper makes little rolls of wax, each tucked up in a folded mopane leaf, in which a single larva hatches and grows. The Heiqum unroll the leaves to eat the tiny wax morsels, which are slightly honey-tasting and are known as 'bushman sweets' by the locals. Heiqum women grind the golden kidney-shaped mopane pods, which glitter with resin droplets, into a fragrant talcum powder. For our part, we too used the mopane tree: its hard wood burns into longlasting and bright embers, and the resin ducts of the burning logs burst in the flames forming fountains and showers of sparks that are fascinating to watch in the blackness of a night. We used a mopane branch as a Christmas tree one year; with its delicate, fluttering, pointed leaves and bright golden pods it needed very little extra decoration. Our son was two months old that Christmas and for his benefit I made small white candles for the tree and strung ribbons of tin foil on its branches.

My favourite time at Okaukuejo was after the camp's light went out at ten at night. We would lie in bed on the gauzed sleeping porch or sit around the bright mopane wood embers of an outside fire listening to the clattering of zebra hooves over the calcrete rubble, their breathless dog-like barks, the rumble and splash of elephant at the waterhole or the thin silvery howl of the jackal quivering through the night air. From the mopane woodlands we would often hear the whistling crescendo of the tiny pearl-spotted owlet or the soft motor-like purr of a nightjar. Pink-fingered, dark-eyed gecko on the house walls would click their jaws and chak-chak to each other. Occasionally we would hear the drama of a lion kill. One night a lion captured a gemsbok nearby and for two hours the dying beast bellowed and groaned.

Very early in the green light of dawn, after a night alive with animal sound, the black korhaan, a hen-sized bird, strutting among the salt shrubs out on the flats around us, would limber up his vocal chords and treat the countryside to the sound that became to our ears so characteristic of Etosha, the raucous and totally unmusical '*so wragtag, so wragtag, so wragtag, o gaats, o gaats, o gaats*'.

3

The Pan

The Etosha Pan or Salina is a dried inland sea or lake which stretches across 8000 square kilometres of the National Park. The plains around the Pan are of white limestone laid down during flooding in ages past. Wild and desolate, these plains are extraordinarily rich in game because of the water which oozes through cracks in the rim of the Pan or bubbles out of sulphurous-smelling artesian wells. Crusts of salt at the edges of the springs and over the bed of the fossil sea are an added attraction to the massive herds that assemble here. Thousands of head of wildebeest, zebra and springbok migrate seasonally around the Pan, grazing the fresh grass found at the numerous brack springs or the miraculous flushes that spring up after brief thunderstorms. Herds of elephant, white-washed by the fine pale calcrete dust, move from Etosha during the wet season into the Kaokoveld mountains and valley plains on the western side of the park and trek back to the Pan again (this time covered in red dust) when the dry season bleaches and denudes the rocky ribs of the mountain country. Although almost a desert, this wide, wild Etosha country supports a wealth of animal life greater than any in southern Africa apart from that in the Rift Valley of Moçambique.

The vast Pan was originally formed by the Kunene River. The Kunene rises in the highlands of southern Angola and once flowed into the Etosha basin, forming a shallow but permanent inland sea that overflowed as its eastern end into the Okavango River. At some stage the Kunene was captured and diverted by another river eating back from the Atlantic coast, and the Pan was left high and dry, fed only by local drainage and a small seasonal river, the Ekuma, that struggles now through the flat, marshy grasslands of Ovamboland in the north. It appears that the Pan was still permanently flooded just over a hundred years ago. Dr. Hugo

Hahn, a missionary travelling in northern Namibia in the 1850s, came unexpectedly across a vast stretch of shimmering blue in the dusty plains. He and his companions could only imagine it to be a mirage, but were informed by a bushman guide that it was indeed a lake that never dried up and that contained great numbers of fish. They later reached the lake, rimmed with flocks of flamingo, and they rode along its banks for many hours.

The Pan nowadays is devoid of water except for deeper-lying areas during the rains. In years of exceptionally high rainfall the entire floor may be briefly flooded. But most of the time its blue-white saline surface lies in frozen wind-riffled sand waves and cracked clay pavements, a pale ghost of its former self. Lawrence Green, in one of his early books on Namibia, *Lords of the Last Frontier*, comments on the enormous size of the Pan and writes that 'all the world's aircraft could land on the Etosha Pan at the same moment without brushing wing-tips'. He also recalls stories told by an old hunter of an 'elephant cemetery' of bleached tusker skeletons sunk into the mud near the middle of the Pan, the very centre of which he maintains no human has ever crossed.

About once every fifteen to twenty years the Pan is converted briefly, after exceptionally heavy rains, into the living sea it used to be; and once again clouds of white pelican and rose-winged flamingo settle in the shallows.

One such year was 1969, the year after we had left Etosha. Thousands of these birds nested and bred along the edges of the flooded Pan. Tragically the waters evaporated and vanished before the young were old enough to fly. The adults eventually abandoned them to save themselves and the desperate chicks started out on foot in long pathetic lines, plodding on and on over the burning white clay, blindly searching for water and their parents. Those that were not rescued by the Ranger staff quickly succumbed to the heat and thirst.

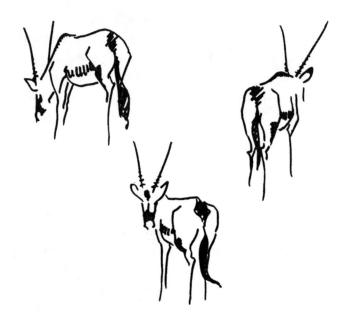

The name Etosha comes, apparently, from a word in the Herero language meaning 'the place of mirages'. On the white-hot days of the dry season the Pan seems as though it could be the very origin of mirages, like the pale eye of a vortex spinning them off one after another. One could almost imagine it to be the birthplace of dust devils too, as so many of these small whirlwinds climb off its burning surface to twist and dance into the sky. Dark ostrich and wildebeest hover and flutter far above the Pan's surface, the heat waves lifting and elongating them into unfamiliar shapes and patterns until they dissolve entirely into the liquid horizon. Herds of zebra flicker whitely, like crystals forming in this liquid, and the blue images of the few *koppies* that emerge from the Etosha plains float above it.

Ken and I were fascinated by this great white desert, and we would often drive out on to it, especially during the dry seasons when the clay surface was not treacherously boggy. To walk out alone over the centre of the Pan always gave me the feeling of being sucked into and submerged by the wild loneliness, so that I became one with the grey stretches, and with the infinite nave of the sky. There was no sound at all; an utter silence seemed to press upon my eardrums and temples, and my body shook with the inner drumming of blood through the veins.

At sunset the clay surface of the Pan is blue-green against a pink sky and the shining freckle of the evening star is the only landmark. On moonlit nights the panscape turns into a crystal sphere of blue and white: the sky and the earth seem to unite in a pale, ethereal orb.

I was fortunate enough to be taken over Etosha in a light aircraft one clear winter's day. From the air the edge of the Pan is seen to be intricately patterned with brown and beige whorls and waves of swash banks left by past floods. Khaki and grey stretches of short grass and salt bush take over where the pale scrolled edge of the Pan leaves off. Game paths interweave over them like the veins of a leaf or the furrowed wrinkles in an elephant's skin. Further away, on higher ground, the grass is taller and conical anthills appear, looking from the air like warts on the skin of the earth. Carpets of grey thorn trees and lime-green mopane alternate according to changes in the soil.

Game often walk over the Pan. Ostrich pace out the dusty distance, the snake-like neck holding a head with far-seeing eyes motionless as the big body rocks to the gait. Sometimes an immature hen will lay an experimental and unfertilized egg alone and white on the white clay. Migrating zebra in single file churn the white to grey as they cross an arm of the Pan on their way to northern grass plains and new grazing.

On the edge of the Pan is a site with the delightful name of Wolfsnes. This place was named after the lair of a brown hyaena was found there some years previously. The brown hyaena is called a *Strandwolf* in Afrikaans, meaning a beach wolf – as they were, and still are in places, fairly common along the beaches of the Skeleton Coast. There they scavenge what seafoods they can and perhaps attack the baby seals that are born in the colony at Cape Cross. The brown hyaena differs from the more common spotted hyaena in several ways. It is much hairier, with a long mane of coarse hair over its back. The ears are more pointed and the general body colour is darker. It is also a much less aggressive animal than the spotted hyaena, living and hunting singly or in pairs and preying mostly on small mammals, carrion and fruit.

Near the old hyaena den and dotted around amongst the scrubby salt bushes were a large number of ground squirrel burrows. The squirrels were quite unafraid of vehicles or people and someone had, as people will, begun the habit of feeding them and so making them even tamer. We would spend long spells watching these vivacious beige and cream-coloured burrowing rodents. They are diurnal and could be seen out of their burrows at almost any time of the day, playing and feeding. Ground squirrels have long tails which they can fluff out at will, but which at rest are rather slender. It seemed to us that the little animals use their tails as sunshades in the hottest part of the day, bushing up the fur and crouching beneath them while they nibble on a root or seed. The tails are used a lot in play, which occupies a great deal of the squirrels' time; they can be flicked or fluffed, flirted or whisked depending on the owner's mood and situation. Ground squirrel holes are sometimes used by ant-eating chats as nesting sites. Larks and pipits on very hot days retire into the burrows as there is no other shade available.

The strange and seemingly empty landscape of the Pan thus has its inhabitants: some minute such as tiny spiders that spin almost invisible webs across cracks in the clay surface, some large and migrant such as the salt-seeking hoofed animals, and many both large and small that live in the salt bushes and grasses around the edge of the white dried sea.

4

Drought and Rain

Namibia, like other arid lands, is a scene of sharp contrasts. The dry winter season is long and harsh with sun-baked earth, desiccated remains of bleached grass, and dark skeletons of dormant trees. The winter nights are sharp and frosty but the days are clear and hot with heat waves rising and the song of cicada sizzling like a vocalization of the heat.

Spring brings wind and dust storms, the atmosphere is brittle and dry, so hot and intense that you feel you can surely not stand another day of it. The woody plants flush and flower in response to warming nights, or to the lengthening days if the bare minimum of soil or sap moisture has been retained, but still the rain holds off. Huge cumulo-nimbus clouds build up each afternoon, towering and prominently dark, and along the horizon purple mists of rain, delicate and remote, evaporate before touching the ground, the sweet wet smell of it sometimes sweeping towards us on the wind.

The game does not appear to suffer from prolonged drought – at least not in Etosha, where the populations are in fairly good balance with their environment and have sufficient room in which to move about. But these – the zebra, springbok, gemsbok, elephant – are all animals that have evolved under continual recurring drought conditions, under the shaping pressures of the arid and semi-arid environment. Zebra have a digestive system that is adapted to obtain the optimum nutrition out of the poorest and coarsest grazing. Springbok are mixed feeders and can raise their heads from the bleached grass tussocks or bared ground and chew protein-rich, dried-out twigs of the salt bushes. Elephant swing heavy front feet to dig out edible roots. But above all the wild herbivores are opportunistic and move to take advantage of the changing conditions in the environment. They move to where rain has fallen and where grass is sprouting, or to vlei areas and riverine strips where no other grazing is available. They may move spontaneously and sporadically, or they may move in tune to ancient rhythms. The movement of elephant for example between Etosha and the Kaokoveld is an age-old and yearly phenomenon. Their passage takes them past Otjovasandu, on the western boundary of the Park, whose hottentot name, Khoabendus, means 'the place where the elephants come through'. Movement is necessary for the survival of many of the large animals in arid areas and unless they can remain nomadic they will overuse their habitat and die.

The weather was unbelievably hot during our first two months in Etosha before the rains brought relief. There seemed to be no way of escaping the baking, burning heat and the dryness that evaporated sweat before it could moisten the skin and cracked our lips and nasal passages until they bled. The air was so devoid of humidity that washing hung out on the line would dry out completely in less than fifteen minutes. One morning Ken and I saw a number of bronze and green European bee-eaters flying with their undercarriages down. They were gliding and swooping in their streamlined graceful manner, but each bird had its little legs dangling quite ridiculously in the wind! Neither Ken nor I had ever seen this behaviour before; we could only imagine that its purpose was to reduce the body temperature. Glossy starlings react differently to the heat: we have seen them stalking around the garden with their beaks open and panting like dogs. (This is called gular fluttering and many species of birds do it.)

Eventually, late in November, after six months of drought, massing clouds converged over Okaukuejo and the first heavy drops of the summer splattered down onto the baked earth raising a scorched tang, like a hot iron on a damp press rag. Rain at last! The relief was tremendous, the oppressive heat broken. We felt like rushing into the cool air to be doused clean by the fat stinging drops, to stand singing and shouting in the sheer luxury of water!

Once it had begun, a good deal of rain fell during our first summer in Etosha. After the first downpour it came softly at night and cloudy days prevented much of it evaporating, with the result that pans of water lay everywhere, caught up in basins of the impervious limestone. Where a few days before there had been bone-dry earth and stony rubble, suddenly there were thousands of pools and sheets of water. These soon

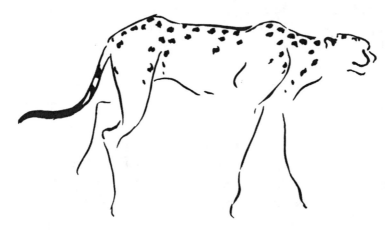

became peopled by small crustaceans, such as fresh-water shrimp, whose eggs lie dormant under desiccated conditions and hatch immediately on being swamped, and frogs which have recovered from their hibernation in cracks and crannies. The little aquatic animals reliant on these ephemeral waters reproduce rapidly, sometimes within a week, before their life-sustaining pools dry up and leave them stranded.

A few days after the first rains our previously bare stretch of garden turned bright with buttercup-yellow *dubbeltjie* flowers. These weeds flourish in overgrazed and bare areas, and the worse the dry season has been, the more spectacular are the *dubbeltjie* carpets! Once the flowering is over the tough three- or four-spined seeds litter the ground and make themselves felt through all but the thickest of boots.

A trip to Ovamboland after heavy rains in the summer of 1965 took us up through the park and the grasslands bordering the Ekuma River at the north-western end of the Pan. Driving slowly along the rough sandy track we came across flocks of birds: storks, herons and yellow-bill kites wheeling in dozens above the thick grass. Some would drop down out of sight and others would rise heavily as we disturbed them. We could at first not see what had attracted the flights of these birds and then suddenly the track ahead of us was covered in a moving carpet of tiny frogs; a veritable plague of them, hopping and skipping across the road. Simultaneously emerged from their infanthood in the rain puddles, they were going we knew not where, but were being eaten up as fast as they went.

One night after the rains Ken and I took Elke Stark out looking for frog species not yet collected or recorded in the Etosha area. Armed with torches, and wearing rubber shoes as protection against the sharp limestone rubble, we searched the edges of the pans. A high pitched and continuous 'rrrrrrrrrr' call enticed Ken into the water up to his neck amongst the trunks of half-submerged trees. He managed to catch the performer, which was quite a feat as the ventriloquial quality of frog calls is notorious. The specimen proved to be well worth the effort as it was the splendidly marked strawberry-pink and black *Phrynomerus*, a new distribution record for Etosha. It has an exceptionally poisonous skin secretion and is related to the arrow-poison frog of the Amazon.

Elke and I could hear no further frog calls except the familiar deep mooing of giant bull-frogs; and we waded about enjoying the velvet blackness of the night, the soft warm water around our ankles and the twinkle of the torch lights on the rippled surface. Waterbirds roosting on a dead tree were disturbed by our presence and they flapped unseen above us. From far away three loud roars sounded, astonishingly like a lion except for the sequence; it was a male ostrich booming out his courtship call.

In the rainy seasons the tracks through Etosha were often a grey soggy mess, slippery in places, thick with mud in others. Vehicles quite often got bogged down, which is one reason why the park is closed to tourists during summer. A spade is a very necessary piece of equipment for digging one's car out of the mud and yet it was surprising how often members of the staff would forget to take a spade along with them.

Hymie Ebedes was one of those people who seemed consistently to forget. I began to believe that he did it on purpose, perhaps because he enjoyed the adventure of being stranded out on the plains. Before the days when two-way radios were fitted to all staff vehicles Hymie spent more than one night out, bedded down in a vehicle that was immovably settled into semi-liquid clay.

On one such occasion he decided to send Josef, a Heiqum tracker who worked with him, back to camp on foot to fetch help. Unfortunately dusk fell before poor Josef was anywhere near camp, and without a torch or a weapon he suddenly became aware that he was being followed by a pride of young lions. There were no trees to climb and the petrified Josef huddled behind a small salt bush. The cubs were almost full grown but obviously inexperienced and just curious – or perhaps not very hungry. As they circled around the man he clutched at limestone chunks that littered the ground and threw them with all his strength to keep the lions at bay. Josef cannot remember how many hours he was harassed by the cats and no one will ever know what would have happened if he had not had the rocks at hand to keep them off; however he eventually arrived back at Okaukuejo a stricken pale grey instead of his normal milk coffee colour!

After the rains Etosha looks a different world. The bare dusty plains become verdant and lush. The thorn bushes are veiled in yellow or green and the mopane's new leaves are pink and lime. The inevitable (if prolonged) drought has again been broken by the inevitable (if delayed) rains, and the cycle of life goes on.

5

A Day in the Hills

North-west of Okaukuejo lies a range of low *koppies* named Othondundu. From the camp these distant blue hills are the only relief on the otherwise flat endless sweep of the horizon. As rocky outcrops of dolomite standing above the white clay and limestone plains they bear a totally different vegetation and bird fauna. The plant cover is denser on the hills, forming woodland and thicket, as compared to the more open savanna on the flats. Different trees occur there, including some unique species. The 'fairy-tale tree' or *sprokiesboom* occurs nowhere else in the world but on the Etosha hills and the Kaokoveld. A few of these weird looking, pale and twisted trees do grow on a patch of rocky limestone plain not far from Okaukuejo, but mostly their home is on the hills.

Once the trees had flushed and flowered after the rains in our first year, Ken and I visited the *koppies* to record what birds we could find there and collect specimens of unfamiliar plant species to send to the Windhoek herbarium for identification. Ken later plotted the distribution of different species from all over the park, helping to produce Etosha's first comprehensive vegetation map.

Before six one bright January morning I packed sandwiches and a flask of tea into a haversack and we set off towards Othondundu. The track to the hills was not one of the tourist roads and it was long and arduous. Rain the previous night had left parts of it muddy and puddled by the craters of elephant footprints; other parts were rocky with limestone chunks that the Land-Rover had to labour over. We travelled mostly through mopane veld, with the lime-green mopane almost the only species of tree for kilometre after kilometre.

No trip through the veld with Ken is ever direct or uninterrupted. He frequently stops to examine some tree or shrub, to see if it is flowering or fruiting or if animals have been eating it, or he might take detours off into the bush to check on changes in the soil or watershed slope. Seeing something interesting he will suddenly screech to a halt no matter at what speed we are travelling. This can be rather disconcerting if one is not accustomed to it, however I have learned to travel with my feet up braced against the dashboard as a precaution! I enjoy these frequent stops as it gives me a chance to draw, and to explore the undergrowth, collecting interesting pieces of wood, grasses, or pods to arrange in pots back home.

On this particular day the previous night's rain had triggered off swarms of flying termites. Termites are extremely numerous over the African savannas and veld, and their fat-bodied flying forms are a delicacy for many predators. Even the fruit-eating animals such as squirrels will not miss up a meal of termites, and carnivores to the scale of jackals and lion will catch them too. The Heiqum collect skin-bags full and eat them raw or roasted over the fire. The sulphur-green giant bullfrog was one animal we saw feasting on the termites that day. This enormous frog, which can grow as big as a soup plate, is a predator to be reckoned with as his diet ranges from insects and other frogs to mice and snakes. I have heard of one that swallowed fifteen young and extremely poisonous cobras!

Creeping out of their burrow at the base of a termite mound, the flying termites were taking to the air in silvery drifts, fluttering away to start new colonies. Two yellow-bill kites swooped down on them and surprised me by catching the insects in their talons and transferring them to their beaks whilst in flight – like two little boys with popcorn!

Further along the track was a column, some three metres long, of black Matabele ants out on a raid. These big ants invade the nests of different species of ant or termite and carry off the young and eggs, as well as any dead or wounded, as food. The column made an ominous rustling, hissing sound as it crossed the bare ground – a sound that presumably keeps the ants together and in formation.

When we reached the hills it was almost midday. The sun was baking down from an almost colourless sky and sucking every scrap of moisture that it could out of the ground and vegetation. The mopane trees stopped at the base of the hills and gave way to pale-barked sterculias, stumpy, yellowish commiphoras and rock-figs. Pans and drainage lines at the foot of the hills bore witness to the little range's importance as a water-shed catchment in the otherwise flat Etosha plains. We saw no game near the water however as the summer rains had filled depressions of all descriptions in many parts of the park and the animals had dispersed far and wide.

Leaving the Land-Rover, Ken shouldered the haversack with our lunch in it. I hopefully assumed that we were about to eat, as my mouth was parched and my stomach quite empty. Two hours and a lot of walking later however, we had still not had lunch. Although I had ceased to feel hungry, my tongue was now clinging to the roof of my mouth from lack of moisture. Ken unsympathetically explained that I must get used to going for long periods without food or water – especially water – as the time could come when we might be stranded and have to survive for several days with only the minimum of supplies. I found after a few more veld trips that I did in fact get used to going without water and could last a full day without feeling the need for it.

The little brown berries of the wild raisin bush (*Grewia*) helped to alleviate my thirst that day on the hills. I filled my pockets with them and sucked them every now and then. It must have been about three in the afternoon, some nine hours after leaving home and breakfast, that Ken relented and chose a tall sterculia tree under which we could sit and eat our meal and drink our tea.

There was little grass amongst the black jagged rocks around us, only shrubs and woodland. The trees seemed to be alive with birds and squirrels. We heard the bubbling call of the Damara rockjumper, a bird that occurs only on the hills, echoing against the rocks. Diminutive white-tailed shrike-flycatchers darted from one branch to another and the busy little tit-babbler chuckled to himself whilst searching the shrubs for insects. Some distance from us we heard a strange melodious whistling. It was a call that was new to Ken and we followed it to see what bird it was. However, the whistler was elusive and seemed to lure us on deeper into the woodlands on the slopes of the hills. Walking quietly through the trees we craned our necks to see where the bird was, but it remained only a flitting shadow and no more. Months later we were delighted to hear the same whistling in the woodlands of the Caprivi Strip, and to find that it was the grey hornbill that produced the charming song.

Whilst following up the unknown whistler Ken suddenly saw a single male lion resting in the shade of a rock fig on a slope below us. He seemed unaware of our presence and after a while got up, stretched, and padded away down towards the plains. I was relieved to see him go as the Etosha lion are renowned for their aggressiveness.

Once the lion had moved off we threaded our way up between the black boulders and thorny undergrowth towards the top of the hill. These dolomite rocks are the remains of a previous seafloor that was uplifted some six million years ago. Ken struck two of the rocks together, producing a metallic ring and a sharp tang of the deep sea mud from which the rock had so long ago been formed. Dolomite weathers into interesting wrinkles and ridges, making it look like old dark and dried out pieces of elephant hide, which is why the Afrikaans people call it *olifantklip*.

Whilst we were climbing the *koppie* our progress was greatly impeded by swarms of mopane bees that whined around us. These tiny insects are only as big as fruit flies, and they are unusual in the bee family as they gather sweat and other moisture from animals to make their honey. They do not sting, but they can be an absolute curse as they are so persistent, even suicidal, in their efforts to obtain the moisture from your eyes or ears, and, if you happen to be squatting trouserless behind a bush, from any other orifice of the body too. Another horror about the mopane bees is that their attentions make it difficult to keep your eyes and ears open for danger in big game country. Walking through the bush you must of course always be on the alert for lion, elephant, or black rhino, not to mention the smaller dangerous animals such as snakes and scorpions. You can only hope that the bigger game is having as much trouble with the little bees as you are yourself. Once we had reached the top of the hill we found that a slight breeze kept the mopane bees at bay and at the same time it blissfully dried the rivulets of sweat that were streaming off us.

On the hillside a small dry stream bed cut through the talus slope, exposing rocks and stones that had long been hidden from the view of even those few human visitors who might come by. As we walked over its pebbly banks and floor Ken picked up a man-worked pebble; a chip struck off during the making of some Stone Age handaxe or arrowhead.

There were several other chips, bulb-shaped on one side, flat on the other, and we looked in vain for a complete tool.

It was satisfying to think of early man at home on these green wooded islands in the harsh arid plains: to think of him as part of the natural landscape, as much an integral part of the earth's crust as the rocks lying baking in the sun, as the lion or the mopane bee. It made me want to shake off the influence and complexities of modern man and his growing disconnection with nature, and return wholly to the warm dark hills; to pull the green leafy blanket over my head and be once again absorbed into man's early participation in the life around him, into his rhythm with natural processes and environment.

To revert permanently to a primitive nomadic and hunter-gatherer existence like that of the bushmen and the pygmies – a life governed by taboos, in which one's chief preoccupation is with food and water – would not necessarily be rewarding for present-day educated man. But for many of us it is important to be able to experience that way of life now and then. Many people actively feel the pull of mankind's roots, still tenuously linked to the cave, and the law of participation. They feel a refreshing of the spirit and a closeness to their origins when they glimpse a sand grouse rustling quietly about his business, or tread and smell the dank soft floor of a green-lit thicket.

Once the sun started to sink and the hills' shadows spread dark and blue across the plains we made our way back towards the car. But my bush education was not over for the day. Ken suggested that I take the wheel and drive back to camp as practice in the not-so-gentle art of Land-Rover driving! I reluctantly agreed to do so and struggled for the next hour and a half to hold the bucking vehicle on the now darkening apology of a track and to double-declutch without stripping the gears. It had been a day to remember; and despite the heat, the dust, the red-faced sweating, and the mopane bees, despite the nightmare drive back in the semi-dark, I found that I indeed looked back on it with great affection.

6

Pirates and Orphans of the Veld

In summer after the rains thousands of fawn and white springbok gather on the lawn-like grasslands around the Pan. It is here that these gazelle drop their young within a few weeks of one another and big nursery herds are formed. One evening while we were on the plains a deep blue thunderstorm was brewing out over the Pan in the east and the sun in the west was brightening the fresh green grass under the feet of one of these nursery herds and the accompanying herd of mothers. As we got out of the car we heard a chorus of croaks, grunts, urps and moos for all the world like a conglomeration of frogs calling in various voices! It was the young springbok and their mothers keeping contact with each other. The mothers recognize their own youngsters' voices from amongst the hundreds of others and so can keep track of them.

Springbok have a delightful behaviour pattern when they are alarmed or excited. They bounce, stiff-legged, as if on springs, and long silky white hairs unfold from the base of their spines to open out into big, conspicuous puffs. This display is called pronking, which is the Afrikaans word for 'showing off'. Baby springbok love showing off and they practise the display with delight, bobbing up and down over the plains like animated white powder-puffs.

The wildebeest also have synchronized birth times and they drop their young at about the same time as the springbok. Wildebeest calves are rust-red in colour, most conspicuous amongst the blue-black forms of the adults, and as they can move as fast as their mothers a few hours after birth they are not kept in separate herds but run with the adults. Unlike the baby springbok, which lies hidden behind a shrub or grass tuft for some days after birth, the wildebeest calf needs no camouflage as he depends on speed and staying with his mother for survival. The

mother wildebeest does not seem to recognize her young's voice as easily as the springbok and so it is vital for the calf to stay at her side. Calves do get lost now and then and these babies usually end up as food for jackal, hyaena or wild dog, all of which frequent the plains at this time of the year to make use of the after-births and the young or weakened animals.

Late one hot December afternoon we and the Stark family had been swimming in one of the deep unsightly pits that had been dug on the plains to provide gravel for the roads and which filled after the rains with soft milky brown water. The salt bush flats and the new green plains stretched far around us, unbroken except for herds of zebra and wildebeest. As we were starting to return home Pieter noticed a pack of smaller animals were heading in our direction. He recognized them at once as wild dog and as we watched they approached quite near to us.

These long-legged, handsomely marked dogs with big round ears are the pirates of the veld – happy, carefree raiders, hunting in packs and terrorizing the peaceful grazers. They have little fear of man and this gang came close enough for us to admire their easy gait, greyhound build, and orange, black and cream colouring. They loped past us and towards a small group of zebra. Surprisingly the zebra rallied; wheeling together they rushed the predators. The dogs left them, and undaunted, trotted on towards a herd of wildebeest. The sun was setting and dark shadows hid the dogs' movements, but the wildebeest had scented them and panicking they raced past us bleating and burping. The sun turned the dust around them to gold and in this, as in an ancient gold-leaf mural, appeared a frieze of humpbacked wildebeest, their young, and then, twittering their bird-like call, the long-limbed dogs running effortlessly in between. The chase flashed on beyond us with drumming hooves into the orange and purple west until we could see no more.

There was little doubt how the hunt would end, however, as wild dogs are extremely efficient hunters and more often than not succeed in running down their prey. They perform a valuable role amongst the herds of herbivores, pruning the unfit or diseased individuals and moving the herds from one area to another, thus allowing the veld to recover from grazing pressure.

Despite their important ecological role and their endearing qualities, such as a tolerant and affectionate social life, these lovely dogs are probably the worst threatened predators in Africa. Apart from the fact that they are very susceptible to disease, farmers and even game rangers wage war against them and they have been shot out or poisoned in many areas.

Another, and very different, predator of the open plains that we came to know was the bat-eared fox. This small silvery animal, no bigger than a fox terrier, has dainty black-stockinged feet, huge black ears and a pointed black-masked face that wears a rather fastidious and disdainful expression. At dusk, especially after the rains, we would often see a pair, or a family, of them with their slightly humpbacked gait running or playing on the plains. Jane Goodall describes a group of bat-eared fox in the Serengeti playing with a Thompson's Gazelle which actively joined in the game! They are nocturnal in habit and mostly insectivorous, although they will apparently take carrion if it is available. An old antbear or warthog burrow serves as their den in which the youngsters are born and reared.

After a particularly heavy rain in our second rainy season in Etosha, Pieter Stark brought home four of these fox cubs. Their burrow had been swamped and he had rescued the little ones. He gave me one of them to rear, and this I managed only with difficulty as they are extremely wild creatures and unless very young do not adapt easily to foster parents. My small pup howled and cried for three days and would not touch food of any description. It was only after I had carried him about my waist in a folded apron day and night for some time that he eventually came to accept me and to take food from me.

Once tame he made a charming pet, playful and affectionate. He was extremely nervous, however, and the slightest noise or disturbance would send him scurrying to his box with his tail down. When in a playful mood his tail was held crooked aloft like a small umbrella handle! As often happens with wild animals reared as household pets he came to a tragic end. Scared by a loud noise one day he bolted, misjudged a jump and broke his back. I had fed him on a diet of pronutro (a nutritionally balanced porridge), mincemeat and what insects I could catch; but probably this had still been insufficient to strengthen his bones, and his little spine had snapped easily. We had him by this time several months and I was utterly heartbroken when Hymie had to give him an injection to put him to sleep.

A young grey hornbill and a down-furred baby hare were two other orphans that I reared during our years in Etosha. The hare was caught and eaten by a genet cat one moonlit night but the hornbill reached maturity with us. He was a very unprepossessing looking bird, with dull grey feathers, a long curved bill and a vacant expression on his face. He was also covered in lice, and having lost most of his tail feathers during his first moult he stubbornly refused to grow them again. He was however very loving and would sit on my shoulder nibbling my ear and showering lice down my back. Or he would flap around the house leaving large white patches wherever he perched. Once he was adult we persuaded him to return to the wild although he obviously found it a poor second best to life with humans.

Many years later a young barn owl was found at a destroyed nest by a group of American visitors and brought to me wrapped in a towel. He consisted of a ragged bunch of white fluff with an indignant look in his dark eyes and a pair of outsize scaly yellow feet. Owl was an extremely rewarding baby to rear and one of the most delightful pets I have ever had. He ate liver and mince from the first, with bits of cotton wool and feathers stuck into it to simulate the feed his parents would have given him. Later we had to catch mice for him and I introduced him to a living one so that he could learn how to deal with it. I didn't realize however that I should starve him for a few days before introducing him to living prey. The first mouse we let loose at his feet took off with impunity whilst Owl blinked at it happily and remained totally unmoved by any predatory instinct. He merely fluffed up his feathers and looked at me as if to enquire if the entertainment was over.

A young friend who was staying with us and I laboriously set more mouse traps and laid them in well-used field-mouse paths in the grass. How difficult it is to catch a mouse when you really need one. For several nights the traps remained empty; but at least an innocent little brown field-mouse was caught. Feeling worse than a murderer I tied a cotton to the mouse's leg and then to a table leg. Now, the prey could not escape. Owl realized something was expected of him this time and after some hesitation attacked and finally ate the poor mouse.

He was an extremely affectionate bird and would utter a purring 'churr' when he heard my footsteps. As I came through the door he would stare lovingly at me and turn his heart-shaped face this way and that as well as upside-down as if to absorb every aspect of his beloved foster parent. If

a visiting dog came near, the owl would fix him with a steady penetrating stare and clicking his beak dive immediately for an attack. Once on the floor he would fluff himself up to twice his size, half open his wings and spring viciously at the dog, talons first.

Even though I looked after a number of young birds and animals, on the whole I did not wish to make a hobby of rearing wild orphans, as

many women living in the bush do. Rather than care for wild animals in what is to them an alien environment, I much preferred to have contact with them in their own habitats as they were going about their own business. But when I was offered a little orphan I could not bring myself to refuse it, so with a heavy heart I would buckle down to the task of being a twenty-four hour nursemaid and mother. This often included giving two hourly bottle feeds or patiently chewing solids, ranging from raw meat to spinach, to force down reluctant little throats. Wild babies out of their element need even more attention than human babies as they have to be tamed and continuously reassured, as well as fed.

The worst part of it all, though, was that once you had gone through all the immense trouble to nurture and encourage the orphan infant to maturity, and had grown to love it with a tenderness that came from the maternal and protective instincts as well as from the joy of the perfection of the little beast and the trust it steadily began to show towards you, a member of a different species, then so often, something tragic would happen and the human foster parent would be left with a broken heart.

In the small human communities of the parks with other houses and families close by, there are not usually large grounds where animals can run freely and safely. Neighbouring families on the whole do not appreciate half-grown wildebeest trampling their flower gardens or mongoose nipping their children and stealing their chickens! So because of irate neighbours, or worse because of injured tourists, tame wild animals often have to be imprisoned in pens, returned to the wild, or sometimes in extreme cases shot.

Returning to the wild can be dangerous for a young animal that has been reared away from its own society and environment, and when in a few cases, as with the barn owl and the hornbill, it did work, I was extremely thankful and yet apprehensive that their strange background would have left them ill-equipped to survive and adapt to life in the bush.

7

The Tiny Antelope

An hour's drive from Okaukuejo along the edge of the Pan brings one to Namutoni, the second of the three rest camps in Etosha. Namutoni is an old fort built in the 1890s by the Germans as a stronghold from which they could keep a check on the hostile Ovambos to the north and watch for the spread of the dreaded cattle disease, rinderpest. Even now, a hundred years later, the fortress is startlingly picturesque. The four square towers with their brilliant white walls and small rectangular windows rise up against the clear Etosha skies. Shadows on the white walls are deep blue. Arched gateways into the rectangular courtyard are closed by heavy wooden gates and a few palms lend a romantic and north African air to the place. Even though the Namutoni fort was inspired by medieval castles of the Rhine it somehow seems right here in the wilderness of Africa. Its clean strong lines and white purity are fitting to the parched scenes of Etosha.

Visitors sleep in the fort, in rooms where the German soldiers used to be garrisoned. A small museum in one of the towers holds mementos of those far-off days. At night from within the thick walls lions can be heard roaring without, and the hoarse honk of flamingo flying overhead to the pans of Ovamboland.

Not far from the fort is a home of the diminutive antelope, the dikdik – delicate blue-grey and tan creatures not much more than forty

36

centimetres tall. It is said their name comes from East Africa, from the Swahili for 'quick-quick'. In Namibia they are found commonly where thicket grows upon a stony floor or river bank, and keep in pairs, or small family groups of three or four, to the shadows and shelter of bushes or trees where they step as lightly as elves over the fallen leaf litter and rubbly ground.

This area near the fort, consisting of woodland and thicket on broken limestone, is the best dikdik habitat in Etosha. Elephant and the bush-loving kudu have pushed down branches and trees, increasing the cover for the tiny antelope, and the larger animals continually browse back the leafy shrubs to near ground level, just where the dikdik can reach it. Plains animals such as zebra and wildebeest wander through the patchy woodland, grazing and opening up the tall grass that would otherwise hinder the dikdiks' movement and the tree canopy overhead protects them from large birds of prey. So, all in all, this is a dikdik paradise. Traffic along the number of tourist roads may deter leopard and other predators in this spot too, an added advantage for the small antelope. It seemed to us that the dikdik actually seek out the roads and enjoy feeding alongside them. It may be that they, like most thicket animals, prefer the edges, known as ecotones, of their habitats, where the plant variety is richer, and the low bushes thickest; or perhaps they enjoy the stimulation afforded by the passing cars! Elephant certainly appear to make use of traffic in this way. Young bulls will often stand near the roads, despite their nervousness, for the sake of a little excitement and the chance of making a mock charge as an outlet for their adolescent frustrations!

We often visited the dikdik as Ken was preparing a report on their behaviour and ecology. (He later published this in the journal of the Nature Conservation Department which is called '*Madoqua*' after the dikdik itself, *Madoqua kirki*.) Four other dikdik species occur in the arid zone of East Africa, but between them and the one in Namibia there are none at all. A geologically earlier arid belt, stretching diagonally across Africa from north-east to south-west, must have allowed the distribution of the tiny animal to reach Namibia; and it was later cut off here when moister conditions eliminated the arid corridor.

The Namutoni dikdik were well used to cars and we could approach to within metres of them. A person on foot however would startle them from quite a distance away. From the Land-Rover, Ken and I would watch while the little blue-grey forms materialized out of the shadows and delicately went about their business as though we were not there at all. The long rubbery proboscis that gives the dikdik its Afrikaans name of *neusbokkie* is agile and sensitive. It twists and bends to catch a scent and thrusts sharply downwards when the buck gives its sharp alarm whistle or soft warbling call. A crest of ginger hair lies back between the sharp prongs of the male's horns and smoothly up the forehead of the hornless female. When alarmed or excited the dikdik raises this crest, which gives it an impish, little-boy-with-a-brush-cut look. Part of the alarm behaviour is a high stotting leap with the fragile tan legs and neck rigid and the blue-grey body as taut as a bowstring.

Like many small antelope the dikdik has huge dark glands just below the eyes. They produce a pungent tarry secretion out of two slits, with which the dikdik marks twigs and grass stalks to advertise the extent of its territory. The pairs are strongly territorial and keep well within their marked plots.

The dikdik's shiny black droppings, not much bigger than those of a rat, are continually deposited in the same sites, so that extensive communal dung heaps result. The Ndorobo of East Africa have a delightful legend about the original reason for these heaps. They say that long, long ago the king of the dikdiks tripped over a pile of elephant dung. He was so indignant and upset that he gathered all his subjects together and decided that in the future all dikdiks would defecate in one place in the attempt to build a dungheap big enough to trip up an elephant and repay him in kind!

In East Africa hunters make use of this habit in order to trap dikdik. They dig a small hole in the centre of a much-frequented dungheap and line it with a ring of thorns pointing in and down. A dikdik stepping into the hole cannot extricate its fragile leg and is trapped.

Dikdik used to be found in thicket areas throughout Namibia, except in the extreme south, north, and north-eastern areas where sand, and not clay and stones, cover the ground. The hooves of the dikdik have rubbery pads on their under-surfaces which appear to be an adaptation to rough broken ground, and it seems that they could not flourish in soft sandy terrain.

Like the gemsbok, the springbok and the camel, the dikdik has no moist black outer skin, or rhinarium, on his nose. This is probably an adaptation to conserve moisture under arid conditions. The dikdik seldom if ever drinks. Like the springbok and the gemsbok he obtains enough moisture for his needs from his food, and possibly from dew or drops of moisture on early morning leaves. Fallen leaves, flowers and fruit form an important part of his diet as they do in the diet of the 'mini-ungulates' of the moist forests, such as the blue duiker and the suni antelope.

The future of the dikdik in Namibia is likely to be secure for some time to come. Thicket and bush, its optimum habitat, is steadily increasing as overgrazing and erosion reduce the grasslands.

Our dikdik, or Damara dikdik as it is often called, is endemic to Namibia and to southern Angola. This species, little different to its cousins in East Africa despite the large gap in distribution, occurs only in these arid south-western reaches and nowhere else in the world. The hills of Etosha and the mountains of the Kaokoveld are veritable treasure

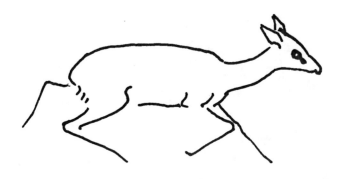

houses of other endemic animals and plants which are unique to these areas. Unlike the dikdik which is comparatively widespread some of these endemic species are confined to only a small area, perhaps to one mountain or mountain range. A great deal of speciation seems to have taken place here: plant and animal populations in the wooded rocky areas have been isolated from each other by the often vegetationless plains, and changed over the generations into different races and eventually different species. A tremendously rich variety of fauna and flora has thus been created, which as yet we know very little about.

8

The Namib Desert

From the interior plains of Namibia lines of savanna trees stretch along stream courses between the wild Kaokoveld mountains and down into the undulating sands of the Namib desert. Water seldom runs on the surface of these stream beds but is often present underground. Elephant and baboon dig through the sand with their front feet to reach the water and by so doing make it available for other animals. Man makes use of these little wells too, enlarging them if necessary.

The lines of trees that grow along the water courses form moister habitats deep in otherwise forbidding surroundings, thus allowing animals like the dikdik, impala, the bush squirrel, elephant-shrews and others to survive and breed in the midst of the desert. These linear oases provide shelter and food for large animals too. As they move from one stream bed to another elephant and rhino plod over many kilometres of barren gravel plains, where the only plant is a tough ancient conifer, the Welwitschia.

I was able to accompany Ken on one of his trips into the Namib and I fell completely in love with it. It has the lure of utter simplicity and spaciousness; and it shows up starkly, because of the lack of vegetation, how the landscape has been created – how it has been shaped, gullied, and flattened by erosional forces. The ancient plains, which have been gnawed at and broken into by rain, flow, and wind over the ages, are reduced to black table-top remnants, or monuments of heaped boulders, while the new infilled plains spread, sloping gently this way and that, far away to meet the sky.

In the sub-desert zone before the Namib proper, the plains are covered in places by a sparse spread of fine tawny grass. This tough-fibred 'bushman grass', so called because it grows in lands once populated by the bushmen, springs up after the rare showers that fall and flowers into silver-white fluffy spikes. It then soon dries and bleaches, and before the end of the winter season it becomes flattened by the wind or by herds of springbok and gemsbok, and it disintegrates and blows away. In the desert itself the plains are naked and white, more planed, less rolling, and covered by a pavement of gravel – wind smoothed and polished.

We followed a faint track, that narrowed to invisibility in the distance, to the Namib Desert Research Station, built on a spot that the hottentots named Gobabeb. The station had recently been established through the efforts of a German desert entomologist, Dr. Charlie Koch, who specialized in the flightless beetles that abound in the Namib. At Gobabeb the white plains end abruptly up against the tree-lined banks of the Kuiseb River. Although dry for most of the year the Kuiseb retains enough moisture under its sands to support a thick growth of winterthorn trees, whose green colouring forms the only darkness in this pastel-pallid world. On the other side of the river tall sand dunes rise up as suddenly as the plain has ended. These giants, pale apricot in colour and stretching in lines right back to the coast fifty kilometres away, never manage to cross the Kuiseb and continue their timeless rhythm over the blank white plains as periodic floods sweep away the slowly encroaching sand.

The Research Station at Gobabeb was established to study the fascinating ecology of this desert which some claim is the oldest in the world, although there is scientific evidence nowadays that gives cause to doubt this.

As we arrived at the door of the small station building we were greeted by an irate elderly figure wrapped only in a large coloured beach towel. 'Who are you?' he demanded, as if to say, whoever you are, go away. Ken introduced us and Dr. Koch reluctantly welcomed us inside. To him we were yet more visitors who would interrupt firstly his bath, and then his precious working hours. However, he warmed to us later; we stayed the night and were grateful that we were able to get to know this colourful and great scientist, especially as he was then near the end of his life.

Exploring the dunes, in the crisp clearness of the next day, we could see a bank of fog in the west being pushed by the morning landbreeze back out to sea. On three sides of us the dunes undulated, becoming copper and then an incredible lilac in the distance. To the north was the vast expanse of empty white plain sweeping on silently and seemingly forever.

The dunes are voluptuous and silken, curved sensuously by the caresses of an ever attentive wind. Some slopes are rippled and grained, others smooth. We walked up a long sloping crest, our feet sinking through the deceiving knife edge of the warm sand. At the top a slight breeze was lifting little veils off the peak and below eddies skimmed and whirled in the hollows. The wind provides food for the surprising variety and numbers of animals that live in the dunes. Seeds, grass, leaves and twigs blown into the desert from surrounding grasslands or oases collect in the hollows and are eaten by the flightless *Tenebrionid* beetles, which in turn feed the geckos, and the rodents – these in their turn being preyed upon by the desert snakes. All these animals have evolved various strange, almost magical mechanisms to enable them to live and move in the deep soft sand, and to withstand the extreme aridity and sharp temperature changes between day and night.

An interesting and important aspect of the Namib is the fog which rolls inland at night in ghostly waves from the cold Benguela current of the Atlantic Ocean. Because of the moisture it provides some animals and plants which could otherwise not live in extreme desert occur in the Namib. Near the coast the desert sands are dotted over huge areas with lichen-covered pebbles, which look from a distance like fields of flowers or grass. Some parts are covered with orange lichens, some with green and some with white, all drawing the little moisture they need from the night fogs.

9

The Caprivi Strip

About a year after we had arrived in Namibia Ken was asked to do an ecological reconnaissance of the Western Caprivi Strip. He was to help determine the future of this piece of country, whether it should be settled by humans or made into a nature reserve. The Caprivi Strip juts like a club from the north-eastern corner of Namibia. The long thin handle, the Western Caprivi, lies between Angola and Botswana and falls under Namibian administration; the club end, the Eastern Caprivi, lies between Zambia, Botswana and Zimbabwe and falls under South Africa. Ken was to ascertain whether the sand country Western Strip was unique in Namibia as far as the fauna and flora were concerned, thus making it eligible for nature conservation status, or if it was better suited to the settlement of 'bushmen' and Okavango tribal people and possible irrigation schemes.

At the time of our visit the Western Caprivi was very little affected by man. There had never been much human settlement there owing to the nutritionally poor white sands; and away from the two rivers, the Okavango and the Kwando, that form its western and eastern boundaries, there was little to no surface water. At that time too it was occupied only by a few bands of hunter-gatherer hottentots belonging to the Kwe and the Mcanigwe tribes. Like the Heiqum, these Nama-speaking tribes are often referred to as 'bushmen' because of their hunter-gatherer existence.

In the autumn of 1966, once the rains were over, we got ready to spend two months in the Strip. The old International truck which was Ken's official vehicle at the time was loaded to the roof with camping equipment, food and petrol. Simon, Ken's Heiqum tracker, and Johannes, an incredibly stupid Ovambo who was working for us at the time and who was to act as cook, were perched on top of it all.

We left Okaukuejo at six o'clock one May morning. There was as yet no light at all and the morning was dense and cold. A slim and delicate sliver of moon peeped out through the thorn trees and myriads of stars pricked the sky's darkness. In the beams of the headlights wildebeest and zebra eyes flashed beside the road and the dark shapes of the owners rocked or trotted away as we approached. A tiny silver fox dashed frantically into the protecting shadows, his brush trailing, long and fluffy, almost bigger than the rest of him. The darkness in the east flushed magenta and then with slow splendour the sky lightened to pink and turquoise, the tiny moon faded out of sight and after the long, almost ritualized phases of changing colours the sun slowly rose. To watch the sunrise from the first crack of dark to the final crescendo of light made me feel a new awareness of the tremendous importance that each individual day must surely have to be heralded by such splendid ceremony.

The rising sun in our eyes, we stopped to see what was causing a cloud of dust beside the road. Two springbok rams pushed in head to head dispute, oblivious of us in their intensity. Most antelope look clean but the springbok is the cleanest-looking animal I know; the shining golden tan of his coat and pure whiteness under the belly are spotless and heightened by the chocolate brown curves along his sides. These two glistening little beings, like horned immortals from Mount Olympus itself, pushed and prodded one another for a few minutes, then the tussle ended in triumph for the smaller of the two who raced after his adversary with flying heels.

It took us four days to get into the Strip as we had to stop *en route* at Rundu, the administration centre for the Okavango and Caprivi Territories. Here we received official permission to enter the Strip and to carry two rifles, one for our own protection and one small calibre for the possible shooting of birds for museum specimens. Plans were made to deliver drums of petrol to us after a few weeks and we were issued with anti-malaria pills and terramycin ointment for the treatment of a prevalent and dangerous eye disease that is carried by flies.

Rundu, called Runtu at that time, is a small sleepy settlement overlooking the Okavango River. The Commissioner or Administrator was the little king there and he lived a gracious life in a large house with

extensive gardens and orchards. Below his well-kept estate on the high bank of the river the Okavango slowly swept past floodplains and thick riverine vegetation. Thin bush cattle grazed the floodplain amongst flocks of black open-bill stork which hunted for their fresh-water snail diet amongst the water plants of the pools. Although bilharzia was rife people fished the pools and poled their dug-outs along the river. Water dikkop and fish eagle called. Pied kingfisher hovered above and dive-bombed their own reflections.

During our few days in Rundu we stayed with the local police sergeant, Steve, who by coincidence had been based in Zululand at the time Ken had worked there and knew him well. One afternoon we walked over to where Steve had told us a bushbuck was being held in captivity. It was a Chobe bushbuck which has a brighter colouring and slightly different markings from the other variety with which we were better acquainted. To our surprise in a large enclosure next to the bushbuck was a family of camels. We were told later that a team of camels was until recently

kept at Rundu for the use of police patrols over the heavy sands of the
Okavango territory. Intrigued by the lumpy, disdainful, and smelly beasts
Ken and I walked up to the fence for a closer look. As we approached,
the tall male gave a gurgling, retching noise and spewed out a length
of bloated, pink, slimy membrane which dangled down the side of his
mouth and then was slowly retracted. The impact of this astounding and
totally unexpected greeting on us was tremendous. We were completely
taken aback and decided that the camel was an even more unfortunate
animal than we had previously imagined!

Months later in the Windhoek library I came across a leather-bound
tome printed in 1884 that had a picturesque explanation for this
atrocious habit. Titled *The Camel: Its Uses and Management*, and written
by a Major Arthur Glyn Leonard, it had the following to say about the
'palatal flap' and about another peculiarity of the camel's that we were
lucky enough to witness that day. 'During the rutting season the palatal
flap of the males alone – an inflated organ which only appears when the
animal is "mast" – hangs from the mouth like a bladder, invariably on
one side only – the near, if I remember right. It never appears until the
animal reached puberty, which is usually in his fifth year. The female,
although she possesses one, never produces it. . . . The nature of this
organ is unknown – at all events, appears to be extremely doubtful - .
. . and yet it must be acknowledged that Nature designed it for some
rational purpose, and that all Nature's handiwork is purely and exquisitely
practical no one will deny.

'Another peculiarity about the camel is the way in which he stales. He
does not discharge his water like a horse or ass in one continual stream,
and have done with it; nor does he stop to do it, but he dribbles a few
drops at a time, and keeps stalking steadily on – then a few more drops,
and so on; and he does this even when he is standing about. Parthey says
that the camel urinates very scantily and does this at regular intervals,
so that Bedouins and Arabs are enabled by this to trace the direction or
route taken by the caravan.'

IO

The Okavango River

Once our papers were in order we left Rundu and bumped along the rough Okavango Territory road to Bagani, where we were to cross the Okavango River into the Caprivi. Millet and maize fields lined the road and turtle doves flew up in front of the car in great flocks. Lines of local women and men with tin dishes of gravel carried on their heads were repairing the surface of the road, providing hardening and filling in potholes. They were cheerful people and waved gaily as we passed.

The village of Bagani was nothing more than a collection of camps, and a reed and thatch schoolhouse where we were to show our note from the Rundu Commissioner permitting us to cross the pontoon into the Caprivi. The schoolmaster left his rows of dark, shiny-faced pupils to come and meet us. He was a tall pleasant-faced black man with whom we were later to become very friendly.

We decided to stay over at Bagani for a few days in order to explore the banks of the Okavango, and we were shown to a camp that had been built for the use of visiting officials: small reed huts with sandy floors in a clearing overlooking the river. From the lush riverine vegetation around the camp came the low, gentle call of the exquisite and inappropriately named Angolan mourning dove. Hardly mournful, its call is in fact a contented purring sound. In contrast, a crescendo of song burst from a thicket where the handsome orange, black and white Heuglin's robin was busy amongst the leaf litter.

This camp had a reed toilet some little way from the huts, unlike the other camps in the Territory where it was automatically accepted that visitors must use the bush as do the locals. I found it was in fact preferable to use the bush even in this case as the 'long drop' pit was in a foul condition and the reed walls housed generations of spiders and insects. Near to the toilet was a hollow tree out of which popped the small, whiskery ginger head of a bush squirrel. He was fairly tame and visited the camp at times during the day to find scraps of food.

Johannes built up a big fire that night and we warmed tinned chicken for our supper. Later, lying on the sandy floor of the hut, we heard hippo hawing and grunting from the river and somewhere nearby an elephant screamed.

The next morning a pearly apricot mist lay on the river and the air was moist and tangy. Wishing to explore the Caprivi side of the river, where there are floodplains, we drove down to the pontoon crossing. The wooden pont was cable drawn and as old and decrepit as most of its kind in Africa. Having driven precariously down the bank and on to the pont Ken and I got out of the car to enjoy to the full the short, slow journey. Crossing a river on a pont is an experience so delightful and romantic that one wishes the pace of our lives had allowed more ponts to survive instead of being replaced by bridges. Above and below us the river flowed wide between dense trees and sandy reed-covered islands; behind, the green water was whipped up by the slack of the cable as the team of ten men pulled and sang. Reed cormorants and divers flew in chains overhead and on the far bank a rusty-feathered coucal, that large bird of the reeds that many name the 'bottlebird' because of its bubbling 'water being poured out of a bottle' call, sat sunning itself in the reeds.

The Okavango is the most beautiful river I have ever seen. It is deep and swift-flowing. The surface, unbroken by rapids or shallows in these stretches, is smooth and serene. Shafts of reeds growing along the edges judder in the current, and can be seen through the clear water right down to the sandy floor where pike and bream swim in amongst them.

A later crossing we were to make on the Bagani pont was under moving masses of storm clouds. The whole experience was to me a symphony in movement. The pont was moving, the river was moving, the wind stirred, the clouds were billowing and converging, and against this dark, moving canvas two fish eagles, far above our heads, soared and twisted in flight.

On this first morning as we left the pont we followed the track that leads southwards along the river. Turning inland the track passes through scrub areas of Zimbabwean teak trees sprouting up on old cultivation sites that have probably been deserted for ten or twelve years. Further on huge acacias and clumps of thicket alternate with open grassy glades. This is magnificent big game country; but despite the many reports we had heard of the quantity of wild life in the Caprivi, we saw very little evidence of it.

The road returned to the river and floodplain a few kilometres further on. Here we caught a glimpse of two reedbuck cowering in the tall coarse grass. The floodplain becomes very wide in this area and its mud flats provide excellent feeding grounds for water birds and waders. We saw flocks of spurwing geese, white-faced duck, egrets, and open-bill storks. Wattled crane and great white heron stalked amongst the reeds and a goliath heron stood against a background of tousle-headed papyrus keeping a sharp eye open for frogs and fish. Further on, the track ran alongside a lagoon which had been cut off from the river. Pastel water

lilies lined the edge and their pads showed deep purple where overturned by wind or current. Jacanas paddled on long-toed feet over and amongst the pads, their bronze bodies bright in the sun. Black-winged stilt lifted knees to their ears while walking jerkily through the mud. A white-winged bird rose up from the reeds – a squacco heron; when it settled again the folded wings and tail showed none of the white so conspicuous in flight and the pale biscuit of the outer feathers blended into the reeds. A perfect vanishing trick.

We drove the thirty kilometres or so to the southern boundary of the Strip and were surprised to see no more game at all. A few metres inside the Botswana border a huge baobab tree raised bare stumpy branches to the sky. Two bateleur eagle settled on the topmost branches like a royal couple seating themselves on a towering throne. A little browny-red squirrel scuttled around the tree's mighty waist and disappeared with a flirt of the tail. Turning west along the cleared strip of the boundary line we came once again to the river, where we stopped for a belated lunch. Opening a tin of peaches, we ate them with whole-wheat biscuits and drank the juice. A yellow barked acacia above us was festooned with a pink flowered mistletoe-like parasite; the flowers and attendant insects attracted sunbirds, white-fronted bee-eater, and blue waxbill.

Back at the pont crossing late that afternoon we had to call and then wait a while for the operators who, when they did turn up, were in such good spirits that from our side of the river we could almost smell the fumes of their favourite fermented sugar-water drink! At last the pont crashed into the bank where we were waiting and a very shaky individual came to spray the car, a precaution against the carrying of tsetse into the Okavango Territory, where it does not occur, from the Caprivi where in the eastern stretches it is common. With cackles of laughter from the crew we then swung crazily across the river which reflected the clear colours of the sunset, the banks on either side of us seemingly hung between two skies.

The local people of the Okavango use dug-out canoes, or *makaros*, on the river. Wishing to visit upstream we borrowed one of these and a man to pole it. A *makaro* is carved out of a solid tree trunk. There is a great deal of work involved and only certain people are able to accomplish it. For this reason a *makaro* must of necessity have a long life and last its owner for many years. If a canoe develops a hole it is either plugged up with sods of earth and grass roots or, if possible, it is left. The *makaro* that we used had a hole as big as a saucepan high up in its side. We had to sit very carefully so as not to rock the boat and lower the hole to waterlevel! As we skimmed along beside the reeds a goliath heron rose from its reflection in the ripples and on vast wings lifted over our heads. Hippo in the middle of the river peeped warily at us, eyes and ears protruding above the water. I watched them with trepidation. A few days earlier we had heard of a rogue hippo (probably wounded) that had attacked a canoe, snapping both it and the man inside in two.

We beached on the Caprivi side at the Popa Falls. *Popa* is the Mbukushu word for cascades or rapids, and these are steep rapids on the otherwise calm Okavango. Curling and curdling, the water rushes over a black outcrop of rock that runs in a straight line across the river. Creamy white banks of sand lie below the rapids, so clean that when we walked over them the sand squeaked above the thunder of the water. Following

a hippo path beyond the falls we sat under a canopy of overhanging branches on the edge of the water: rivulets curled between clumps of ferns and reeds and gnats hung in the air. The damp smell of the river and spray cooled our nostrils and on a sand bank on an island opposite us a large green-black crocodile crawled glistening out of the water to flop inertly in the hot sun. Near him a darter spread her wings to dry, coiling her snake neck to look about whilst the water dripped off shining wings. There was absolutely no sign that a human being had ever been there, except a rough and overgrown track through the trees.

On foot we followed this track which ran northwards away from the river. Guinea fowl flocks ran in spotted haste before us, rattling their alarm tattoo and raising their feathers in agitation. Red-billed francolin also scurried ahead, necks erect, short legs working double time.

This part of the Caprivi is thick bushveld – ideal impala country. We saw many signs of them, but none of the animals themselves. The grey-brown thorn bushes had sparse yellow grass straggling beneath them. We picked and ate raisin-tasting *Grewia* berries to quench our thirst. Rock outcrops occur here in the otherwise rockless Caprivi and on one sheet-eroded rise we found many stones worked by Stone Age man.

Walking down towards the river again and on to the floodplain we saw a herd of elephant standing near the water's edge in the long tawny grass. We approached as close as we could to take photographs and observe what they were eating. The local man who was with us stayed behind. He said his wife was pregnant and according to his people's beliefs he must during this period not go near elephant as they would scent him out very easily and charge! We could not see the herd from the track because of dense bush, so by way of a game path we made our way through to the grasslands. The grass too was tall and we had to talk almost to the water's edge before seeing the elephant properly.

There were ten of them standing about fifty metres from us, quite unaware of our presence. The wind was in our favour and we caught their strong musty, grassy smell. The herd went on feeding quietly and drinking from the water near by. Pulling at clumps of dry grass, they thrashed it around in their trunks for a while before putting it into their mouths. Apart from the dry rustle and swish of the grass they were quite silent – only occasionally a low liquid rumble would come from a throat or a *whoosh* of an ear beating the air. Completely at their ease, although wary for any sound or scene, they moved around slowly and idly, butting each other with foreheads or tusks. Two particularly playful young males engaged in mock combat and the dull clash of the tusks came clearly to us. These two put in a bit of mating practice too, attempting to mount one another. Soon the herd began filing one by one away through the grass and towards the bush. I was anxious, once they were out of sight, that they might come up through the long grass behind us. After they had moved off amongst the trees we heard several sharp, rending cracks as branches were torn down; and twice one of the animals trumpeted – a loud, restless sound as clear as a strident bell, shattering the quiet of the warm African afternoon.

II

People of the River

The Mbukushu and Okavango tribes that live along the Okavango River are Bantu people who came down in the last two hundred years from Angola in the north. The women of these tribes often wear long strands of sisal or sinew woven into their hair to make locks that hang down their backs. The daughter of the pioneer hunter and explorer of the late 1800s, Fred Green, claims that this attractive habit was first adopted by the wives of the chiefs who greatly admired her mother's long straight hair and wished to simulate it.

The women still dress in their traditional costume of short aprons or skirts made of skin or cloth. Beadwork adorns their hair, arms and ankles, and their breasts are left bare. Many of the men of the tribe leave their homes for years at a stretch to go and work in the mines in South Africa. Nowadays they mostly dress in Western clothing, and sunglasses, or safety pins through their ears, have replaced traditional ornamentation.

The Mbukushu and Okavango are both traditionally fishing-cultivating cultures. They grow crops of millet or maize in small plots near to the river, and although they may raise a few goats or cattle their protein generally comes from fish. The women catch fish with scoop baskets woven from pliant twigs and sisal. Carrying these large peaked baskets down to the river on their heads like oversized hats they collect at the shallow pools on the floodplain with their babies and small children. Walking into the water a woman will scoop her basket deep down amongst the waterlily stalks and pull it up to haul her catch out by hand and throw it into a nearby canoe or onto the bank. A 'thrust basket' may also be used. This is a smaller basket which is held by its peak and thrust mouth-down into shallow water. The angler then reaches into the basket through a hole at the top to take out any captured fish.

The men form fish drives with their *makaros*. Forming a small square or circle in the river with four or five dug-outs, they gradually close up, driving shoals of fish together between them where they can easily be speared.

The other people who depend upon the Okavango River for their livelihood are the Mcanigwe 'bushmen' who subsist mainly on fish and waterplants. These people, like the Heiqum and the Kwe, are of hottentot extraction and speak a hottentot dialect. We saw only one group of the Mcanigwe as they live far from the Bantu settlements. They lead a nomadic existence, moving up and down the river and into the swamps along its edges. The group we saw were slender and small statured. Their skin was a warm apricot yellow and their little faces were delicate and heartshaped. The women had streaks of charcoal on their eyebrows, giving them a whimsical air. None of the group could speak a word of Afrikaans, English, or Fanigolo and they were rather shy of us. Reluctantly they showed us a beautifully woven fishing net that they were making. A wrinkled little old man sitting nearby was preparing thread for the net from the bark of baobab and sansivieria leaves. Rolling the fibres on his thigh he produced long tough strands, which were later to be dipped in a preservative dye made from the roots of the *Euclea* shrub.

The Kwe people are similar to the Mcanigwe but they are hunter-gatherers rather than fisher-gatherers. One morning we met three Kwe women on the road to Bagani. Their yellowish skin was darkened by dirt and sunburn and their naked breasts hung dry and limp against their skinny chests. They were carrying huge bundles on their heads, presumably moving house, and we offered to give them a lift. Two women had babies slung across their backs. All three wore skirts of skin and cloth, and sandals made of leather with thongs between the toes and behind the heel. They disembarked a little further along the track, where we met their husband. Unlike his wives he was not wearing traditional clothes, but a dirty green pullover and khaki shorts. He carried a three-legged pot slung on a stick, and a bow and quiver of arrows hung from his shoulder. He was a proud old man, dignified and genteel. Ken asked about the materials from which he made his bows and arrows. He told us his bow shaft was made from *Dichrostachys*, a very thorny shrub that grows particularly on areas of old cultivation and can form dense thickets. The bow-string was the spinal sinew of a steenbok. The arrows were slender shafts of the *Grewia* bush tipped with steel heads that had poison on them from a crushed insect pupa (the real bushmen, the Kung, use the same poison). The shaft feathers, he told us, were from a vulture. Pieces cut from the pinions of vultures are supposed to be aerodynamically perfect for the flight of arrows. The instruments were all beautifully made and the arrows were carried in a large dark quiver of kudu skin.

12

A Visitor in the Night

Halfway from Rundu to Bagani was a trading store where over the months whilst we were in the Okavango Territory and the Caprivi we used to stop to buy provisions. The store was run by an elderly South African couple, Mr. and Mrs. Oosthuizen, who would greet us warmly and no matter what the time of day produce chilled bottles of the Angolan-made beer – Cuca.

This bush store was typical of its genre. The simple brick building was roofed with corrugated iron and had the inevitable and badly painted Joko tea advertisement on its once white walls. Youths and mongrels lounged among old petrol barrels and flies outside the store. Inside it was cool and dark, smelling of cardboard, cloth and human sweat. Shelves behind the counters were covered in tins, bottles, stacks of cheap materials, alarm clocks, paraffin lamps, buckets, blankets, sweets and candles. Black cast-iron three-legged pots stood in towers on the floor next to a row of large open-mouthed sacks, out of which sugar, meal or groundnuts could be ladled. Dusty footprints patterned the concrete floor. A ragged queue of customers at the counter stared at us as we came in: the women had babies suspended from their backs or left hips and their flat breasts hung dusty and limp.

Near the store was the Catholic mission station of Andara. We visited the young German priest there one day as Ken had promised to give him the names of some fast-growing indigenous trees suitable for planting in the mission grounds. We hoped too to be able to obtain information about the history of the tribes in the Okavango area. The mission is situated on the banks of the river. Like the others we had seen, it was cleared of all natural vegetation except a few trees and the ground was swept bare down to the beige-coloured sands. Red-brick buildings with purple bougainvillea clutching and shrieking at the walls made up the residences and the school rooms. The church, red-brick without the bougainvillea, was sturdy with a tall square bell tower. Young girls in fresh, bright-coloured cotton dresses which showed up the shining darkness of their skins dotted the grounds and as our car approached the Father appeared at one of the doorways.

A solid-looking young man with questioning eyes, he invited us in for a cup of coffee. The dining room was stark and cold with linoleum on the floor and a long wooden table down the centre; the remains of breakfast on heavy white crockery decked the table. Brightening up the room considerably were three lovely prints of two watercolour landscapes and one seascape in oil.

We were introduced to a young black priest who had recently been ordained in Pretoria and was on a visit to his home country before returning to South Africa. This man spoke excellent English and was obviously well educated. He listened politely but without much interest as Ken spoke of his sorrow at the rapid disappearance of the black man's culture in Africa. What did this African Catholic priest think of the manner in which the unique and ancient traditions of his people were being drowned by the wave of Westernization, on the crest of which rode such eagerly sought after, but empty, symbols as portable radios, sunglasses and cigarettes? Perhaps he was shy, or wary of showing his feelings, but more likely, being brought up and educated in the white man's way, he had come to accept the loss as something inevitable, progressive, and hardly to be mourned.

The priests were unable to help us with any historical literature on the tribes in the area. The only work of this sort done at Andara was a set of two volumes on the 'concept and aims' of marriage in the Okavango tribes! It is tragic to think of the lost opportunities for studying and recording the tribal life and customs that are now disappearing.

We spent that night at the Andara camp on the banks of the river, above a weir. Huge trees surround this lovely camp and it is filled with the gentle sound of the river. We built a small fire for cooking and then let it die down as there were unlikely to be wild animals in this populated area. Simon and Johannes went off to one of the other huts to sleep. It was a still and sultry night and as there was no danger of hyaenas we decided to sleep outside. I arranged our bedding flat on the sand

under the thatched veranda of the reed hut in which we had put our belongings for the night. Mosquitoes buzzed around us and Ken hung a white mosquito net over our mattress like a tent, to protect us from the ravenous insects. The sound of fruit bats and the murmur of the river soon lulled us to sleep.

Deep in the night after a late moon had risen some sixth sense woke Ken. After years of sleeping in the open Ken's 'danger' sense seems to be more highly attuned than most people's and the slightest strange noise or smell will awaken him. Not two paces from our mattress a man was squatting in the sand, peering through our mosquito net. Ken stirred nothing except his eyes and watched to see what the man would do. After a few moments he had still not moved but continued to stare at us and Ken asked in a low voice, '*Wat soek jy?*' – what do you want? Like a dark streak the figure leapt into the air and in a few bounds was gone into the bush. I awoke as Ken yelled after him but saw nothing except a shape dashing away through the moonlit shrubs at the edge of the camp-site.

The following morning we could see from the tracks in the sand that the man had come straight towards our bed and had sat on my side before moving around to Ken's side. Ken and Simon followed his tracks to their source and were surprised to find that they appeared to come from the Chief's *kraal* or homestead. After meeting the Chief and telling him what had happened, they saw a young man of the same build and wearing the same sort of clothes as our intruder. Ken had little doubt that this was he. On being questioned he appeared afraid but denied having been out of the *kraal* that night. So we never discovered for certain who it was that had been so intrigued by the sight of two white strangers asleep behind a mysterious white gauze curtain.

At this time our vehicle began to give trouble. Determined not to go all the way back to Rundu to have it repaired, we decided to sneak over the border into Botswana and travel the thirty or forty kilometres to Shakawe, a small administrative village, where we had heard there was a garage. We had no money on us so we had to borrow ten pounds from the school teacher at Bagani in order to pay for the repairs.

The schoolteacher was not the only friend we had made in Bagani. A large dark-skinned Mbukushu by the name of Marawe Simbonde had answered Ken's enquiries for a person knowledgeable in the local names and uses of plants who would be prepared to work with us. Marawe and Ken took an instant liking to each other and could communicate quite well in the *lingua franca* of the South African mines, Fanigolo. This is based on the Zulu language, in which Ken is fluent, and Marawe knew Fanigolo from years of working in the mines.

Marawe would perch on top of the vehicle as we struggled along rutted sand tracks and thump loudly on the roof when he spied an interesting tree or animal. The times Marawe would thump loudest however were whenever we were passing a *kraal* belonging to a friend or relative of his. He would then politely enquire of Ken if he could pop in for '*lo* one cup' and ten to fifteen minutes later he would emerge very much the merrier and we would continue on our way. Marawe was eager to accompany us into Botswana as he apparently had numerous friends there.

It was an exciting trip down the old sand track running south. Whilst still in Namibia territory we saw no signs of habitation, and for some twenty kilometres we drove through sandy open woodland and acacia thickets growing on drainage line clays. Fire had swept through a great deal of the woodlands and charred stumps and dead leaves, scorched russet, littered the white sand. We came across a roan antelope that galloped away as fast as it could, expecting bullets no doubt to come whizzing around it. Later a group of vulture and Marabou stork perched in a tree caught our attention. Upon investigating we found a kill that had, according to Marawe, been made by a leopard.

The entrance to Botswana was marked only by a pole gate and a black man in attendance with a book that Ken had to sign. Within the once-British Protectorate the signs of habitation increased and soon we were passing scores of grass and pole huts beside the road. Paths, made by the primitive timber sledges that are pulled by oxen or donkeys and used for transporting barrels of water or sacks of grain, criss-crossed the woodlands.

Shakawe is situated in an exceptionally beautiful spot on the banks of the Okavango where enormous wild fig trees overhang the serene green surface of the river and banks of shaggy-headed papyrus. The settlement is typically European and is marked by the usual planted rows of jacaranda and other alien trees. The square buildings are white and conspicuous, and numerous donkeys, chickens, and goats roam in between them. We introduced ourselves to the sergeant at the police station and then took the car to the garage which stood beside the river, flanked by fig trees and an enormous sausage tree bearing its pendulous fruits.

Our interlude at Shakawe was interesting particularly because of the people we met there and our reaction to them. No doubt we had become 'hermitized' and less tolerant; but after our weeks of simple, isolated and stimulating life in the bush we were exasperated by the confined mentality of the white inhabitants here. Their talk consisted almost entirely of gossip about the other white inhabitants and of their drinking prowess! This kind of attitude I suppose can be expected in any small remote community. But I did find it amazing that although these people were living in a natural paradise they imported *everything* from the outside world. Their food, their recipes, their clothes, their plants, their music, their books, their interests, even their Siamese cats had been brought *into* this delightful little Eden, so that their minds were filled with their own importations and they could not see the interest, beauty, or value of that which was indigenous. I was left in the company of one of the women whilst Ken went to see about the car. She was small, thin and middle-aged with bleached badly cut hair and an over-painted face. An obviously intelligent and well-read person, she was now a wreck – and a drunk. Her fourth gin and soda of the morning stilled her shaking hands but put an end to our already one-sided conversation.

In later years I was to see many examples of the effects that living in remote areas has on white people. These effects are most marked on women, who, unless they have some particular interest or hobby, find it hard once their children have gone off to boarding school to adapt to what they see as an alien, and often frightening, environment. Their loneliness and boredom can become an acid which eats into their souls and bodies. It seemed to me strange that some of these women who obviously need company, parties, and their own culture should continue to live in the bush. Possibly they do so for the very reason that it is their husbands' life and they have no wish to break up their marriages; perhaps they enjoy the romanticism of it as seen by other people – they always have tales to tell of their lonely and often tough existence; or possibly, despite all, the bush has a magnetic pull that will not let them go.

On our way back to Bagani from Shakawe we stopped in a Sambiou Mission to enquire once more about the history of the tribes. Sambiou was even more stark than Andara, the earlier mission we had visited, swept clean of all but the footprints in the sand. A line of *mangeti* trees planted in a stiff and unnatural line spread their bared branches against the wall of the church. A short frosty-haired man in baggy grey flannels and a blue faded shirt, at the throat of which showed a thick woollen vest, greeted us at the screen door when we knocked. We realized that this must be Father Hartman, missionary at Sambiou for over forty years, who had taken a great interest in the histories of the surrounding peoples. Peering at us with pale benevolent eyes from behind finger-smudged spectacles, Father Hartman lisped in heavily accented Afrikaans that he would be happy to tell us something about local tribal history – and to show me the basket work produced at the mission which I was interested in seeing.

We followed him across the yard under the bare *mangetis*. An African woman with a sweet brown face, dressed in the grey drapes of a Catholic Sister, went to look for the key while Father Hartman asked if we would like to see their pet monkey. A tiny grey face peeped out from behind the sacking curtain of a box nailed on top of a pole beside the church. Pulling

the curtain aside with a quick nervous little movement the monkey gave us a closer look and then clambered down his pole, a thin chain clinking behind him. I felt desperately sorry for the little creature, not yet half grown. His grey fur was dirty and bedraggled, but as is always the case with monkeys, his small puckered face was eager and bright, alive with curiosity.

Turning away from the lonely monkey we followed the Sister, who had found the key, into a dark room, cold and smelling of dust and disinfectant. A large brown cupboard held the baskets which are made by the girl pupils under the supervision of the Sisters. They were woven very beautifully from sisal, mostly in the simple brown and red geometrical patterns traditional in this part of Africa; but a few had flower and animal designs that showed a Western influence. Outside in the bright midday sun on an unstable wooden trestle table three young girls were sewing busily on hand machines that rattled and whirred.

Pleased that we were interested in tribal history, Father Hartman took us to the little museum that he had built up. Ken was fascinated to see here an amazing array of Stone Age tools: finely chiselled arrow-heads and silcrete hand axes lay in neat order in several glass cases. This was evidently Father Hartman's love: his lisp became much more animated and his eyes bright as he described the exhibits. They had been found along the river banks where outcrops of the quartzite-like silcrete occur in otherwise rock-free sand country; and their discovery underlined the age of the Okavango river – unchanged except in level over millenia. The museum contained many other interesting pieces – beautiful examples of basket and bead work as well as wood carvings decorated long wooden shelves – and amongst them were natural history exhibits such as a clutch of empty crocodile eggs, small tortoise shells, amber and brown, and a few specimens of dried plants. Above us on one of the walls hung pelts of both species of otter that occur in the Okavango River, the clawless and the smaller spotted-throated variety. Next to these hung the horny shell of a scaly ant-eater and a small leopard pelt.

Father Hartman locked the museum carefully behind him, returning the keys to a native Sister who was practising on an organ in the next room, and led us to the dining-room for a glass of lemon juice. This room was as stark and spartan as the one we had seen that morning at Andara. Dark and tall-ceilinged with a lined floor it appeared to forbid any talking above a whisper. I started when Father Hartman pulled out a cigarette and lit it, obviously to the disapproval of the gloomy room and the huge old-fashioned clock that ticked loudly from the wall. Sitting down at the table we sipped at glasses of tart home-made lemon syrup and water and the Father told us stories of how the Okavango tribe had come into the territory. Like the Mbukushu they had come from the north, from Angola, as recently as the eighteenth century. No one seems to know who occupied the area previously. One story the old man told us was of how the native chiefs, once they had taken over an area either by warfare with the former inhabitant or simply by moving into unoccupied territory, used to mark the spot of their main *kraal* by planting the seed of a large tree. This he explained is why trees uncommon in an area are sometimes found isolated from all of their kind. The lone, gigantic baobab that we had seen on the border between Botswana and the Caprivi was perhaps one such tree.

It was difficult to understand much of what the old German priest told us as his voice was thick and he spoke in strongly accented Afrikaans. Ken and I were shivering in the chill of the unfriendly room and Ken asked if we could write to him and obtain a summary of the history – written in German if it was easier for him, as we could get it translated.

We left the mission with armfuls of very welcome oranges and grapefruit which the Father had given us, and travelled out into the evening toward Bagani. In the west the sky was deeply crimson after the disappearance of the sun, silhouetting the spiky forms of the thorn trees and throwing them up into a relief as black as charred stumps before a fire.

13

Sandveld Journey

After our reconnaissance of the area around Bagani we packed the car for the trip into the Caprivi. We planned to establish our next camp at Bwabwata, halfway along the Strip.

The Western Caprivi is about one hundred and seventy kilometres long and only thirty-two kilometres wide. It is an undulating sand country with the dunes originally wind-formed into lines almost perfectly parallel to each other. The dune ridges are now covered in tall dry woodlands, mostly Zimbabwean teak, while the troughs are under grass or seasonally marshy drainage lines.

Originally one track ran the length of the Caprivi; but when we were there the boundary lines on all four sides of the Strip were being opened up by a bulldozer and the churned earth with half-submerged roots and branches was preferable to the agonizing sand corrugations (which are more like regular waves than short corrugated ripples) and the deep treacherous soft patches of the old track where a vehicle can so easily get stuck. However, on neither the boundary line nor the track could we pick up enough speed to change out of second gear. Grinding along kilometre after painful kilometre I could not imagine that any vehicle had ever been subjected to quite so much jolting. Between Ken and me on the front seat we had the camera case, binoculars, a rifle, a thermos flask, and anything else that was considered too fragile to be put into the back. With every bump these various objects shifted and jabbed me in some sensitive spot or other until I felt black and blue all over.

We had crossed the pont before sunrise and once we were well onto the northern boundary track the sun rose, tipping the autumn *kiaat* trees with gold and flushing the trunks of *shivi*, *mangeti* and Zimbabwean teak. The air was crisp and sharp. Swathes and sheets of tall dry grass beside

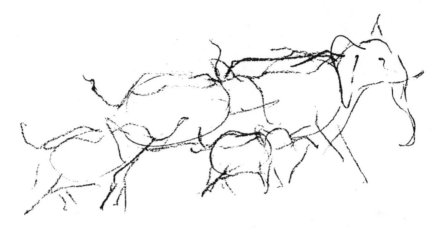

the road and beneath the trees blazed bronze with a richness of colour that is bleached in the light of the older day. Birds started to appear, prinias flicking in the scrub and yellow-bill hornbills flapping from beside the road, one with what appeared to be a lizard hanging from its beak. A black-shouldered kite preened herself on the tip of a dead trunk, her pearl breast dazzling. Parrots screeched in their quick flight, and red-winged shrikes and thrushes fled in front of the car. Further on we saw ten roan antelope and a small group of very frightened elephant rushed, with tails in the air, into the bush on the Caprivi side.

It took us almost a full day to travel the eighty-odd kilometres to Bwabwata. Here there was a reed-walled native *kraal* and another camp set up for visitors. Like the Bagani camp this consisted of three reed and thatch huts and was set in a sandy clearing in the woodland. The huts overlooked a wide, rank-grassed drainage line that was autumn-bronze and dry. A huge sand-mopane which the local people name *shivi* stood in the middle of the clearing, casting a dense shadow from its thick bottle-green crown. The smooth trunk of this tree is a salmon-pink to flesh colour which contrasts handsomely with the dark foliage. The seeds of the *shivi* are delightful too – they are scarlet in colour and when ripe hang from their dry, opened pods by springy yellow threads or funicles.

Bwabwata was home to us for the next two months. We threw a tarpaulin over the sandy floor of one of the huts and spread out the foam rubber mattress and our sleeping bags. One of the other huts housed Johannes and the third the provisions, equipment, and a plentiful supply of starving mice. A fire was built in the middle of the clearing near the *shivi*. Here Johannes and I made stews from the local tough, skinny fowls, thick maize meal porridge (*putu*) and other simple meals. In the hot sand under the coals I often baked bread in a cast-iron pot or a battered tin saucepan. Coals and ashes heaped on top of the tightly closed lid ensured that the loaf came out crisp and brown all over after only fifteen to twenty minutes. I would mix the bread dough in the evening and leave it to rise in a basin on the front seat of the car; the mice would have attacked it if I had left it in one of the huts. The next morning I would form and bake the breads.

One morning two of the policemen who used to patrol the Caprivi's borders at intervals in those days before troop occupation of the territory dropped in and were taken aback to find the homely sight and smell of nearly baked bread under the shade of the *shivi* tree of Bwabwata. They demolished my day's baking with the last of our jam but made up for it on another occasion by bringing me a fat mouse which they had caught and put in a teapot for safe-keeping. Shades of Alice. The fat mouse (that is its official name), is a short-tailed variety of bush mouse. Ken and I had a good look at it before releasing it again into the bush. The same policemen once saved our skins by suggesting that Ken fill our vehicle's punctured clutch fluid box with cooking oil until we could get back to Rundu to have it repaired.

At night at Bwabwata we built up the fire with huge logs to keep us warm as we sat eating supper and writing notes. The autumn chill grew stronger over the weeks and we huddled closer to the flames every night with our fronts roasting and our backs frozen.

The *kraal* at Bwabwata belonged to people of the Mbukushu tribe. David was the headman and the local administration representative. David was his European name and we never did hear his tribal name. We were surprised to find so urbane an individual out here, wearing a dark suit and speaking good Afrikaans! The camp, drums of fuel, and a small first-aid outfit were under his care and the people in the *kraal* appeared to be his numerous wives, children and relations. There were also satellite settlements of Kwe 'bushmen' who were working for the Mbukushu in return for sugar, meal, or tobacco. Many of the women and most of the children had apparently never seen a white woman before and I found them uncomfortably curious. After close scrutiny they didn't appear to be very impressed by this example of white womanhood, as with my short dark hair, deep suntan, shorts, and *velskoen* shoes, I couldn't have looked very white or very woman either!

The emaciated Kwe, in cloth or skin loin-cloths or aprons, often sat around silently observing us or waiting for a handout of tobacco. A young boy with limbs like a grasshopper's performed on his thumb xylophone or *thisjangi*. He played, as these 'bushmen' did everything, lethargically and unenthusiastically. The tune flowed simply from his thumbs, lazy, cheerful, but nostalgic.

The group of native people who lived around us at Bwabwata seemed to be frozen somewhere between their old tribal way of life and a slightly Westernized existence completely incompatible with their environment. They were not gaining much advantage from either. They did very little work and their fields of millet in the poor white sands were neglected. They kept some pigs and poultry but no other livestock. They did not appear to hunt very actively, but then there was obviously not much game to be caught as it had, apparently, been almost totally annihilated by white hunters and police border patrols. We did find one native-set trap line, a barrier of branches and bushes with a noose at the only opening, and one day in the middle of a daily-used path from the *kraal* Ken unsuspectingly prodded a disturbed patch of earth only to have a huge and rusty gintrap clamp itself viciously on to his finger! Fortunately old age made its grip less powerful than it should have been. We pried it off and treated the wound, which healed cleanly but left a nasty scar as a warning to both of us against such incautious investigation.

The only regular food gathering we saw at Bwabwata was done by the women: they collected bundles of fallen *mangeti* (or *mugongo*) nuts, which are produced by the tree *Ricinodendron rautanenii* (a relative of the castor oil plant). *Mangeti* have a very high protein and fat content, and indeed form the staple diet of the hunter-gatherer people in the northern Kalahari sand country lying to the south of the Caprivi. The Kwe at Bwabwata used oil from the *mangeti* to rub on to and cleanse their bodies, water being at a premium. In the heat the oil soon turned rancid and gave the people a lively and nauseating odour – particularly at close quarters!

The piles of *mangeti* were first dehusked and their dry fleshy coats cooked up into a porridge. The nuts then had to be laboriously cracked; the extremely hard shells seemed to yield only to a particular blow

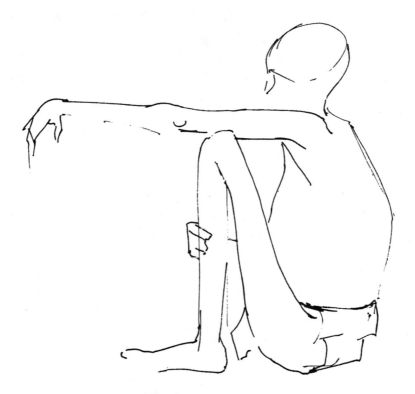

delivered by a particular sharp instrument at a particular spot. The shelled nuts are delicious, like strongly flavoured walnuts. We were amazed to find, years later in Gorongosa in Moçambique, that although there were an abundance of *mangeti* trees growing on the sands there, the local people very seldom made use of the fruit as it was too much effort to crack open the shells. So despite the fact that most of these people have protein-deficient diets the nutritious *mangeti* lie in swards on the sands, and those that do not germinate eventually rot.

The people of Bwabwata led lazy lives, gathering just enough veld foods to keep themselves alive until the regular government-aid lorry delivered sacks of maize meal to them every few months. They had grown to expect this food aid once it had started – although goodness knows why it had – and to complain if it did not arrive. They felt they did not need to help themselves; the government would feed them, and in fact it did. They expected unearned handouts of tobacco, sugar and salt from visitors too, and were peeved if their requests were not granted.

We caught glimpses of the old vibrant tribal life now and again. Some nights, particularly if the fermented sugar drink was available, the deep voices of big drums would start to throb within the reed walls of the *kraal*. One moonlit evening David invited us over to watch the dancing. The *kraal* was unlit apart from an untended fire that smouldered darkly behind a circle of stamping, clapping men, women, and children. The moon behind a thin layer of clouds spread only a cold blurred night, reducing colours to greys and black and white. The compulsive rhythm beat its way into our veins. Women and children sang in high sweet voices and within the circle individuals took turns at dancing. A tall well-built man, a brother of David's, was passionately beating two drums, a large male voice and smaller female voice. Carried away by the beat he leapt up and with a big broad male drum clenched between his knees danced and played at the same time. A girl with glossy bare breasts and shoulders, and a short beaded skirt skittering at her hips, joined him, singing in a loud husky voice and enticing him on after her around the ring. Far into the night the uninhibited drumming, stamping, and singing continued, even the young voices of the children chiming in long after we had turned in to sleep.

14

Counting Trees

Whilst at Bwabwata we started on a complete reconnaissance of the Strip. Ken wished to travel its length and breadth in several transects to ascertain the numbers, more or less, of large game (although we had by now become resigned to the fact that there was very little) and to do analysis samples of the various habitats such as the Zimbabwean teak woodlands, the riverine woodlands, and the rather small localized areas of thornveld. Analysing these plant communities for dominance of species, denseness of cover, and various other factors entailed marching in a determined manner exactly forty-four paces and then stopping and recording details of every tree and shrub within sight and every grass and weed within a wire metre-square quadrant that Ken laid at his feet. While he occupied hour after hour with this scintillating pastime, I followed slowly after him amusing myself with bird-watching or drawing.

In big game country Ken needed someone besides me to accompany him and to watch for danger whilst he applied himself to his data collecting. In the Caprivi, Simon or Johannes was always with us. That danger often crops up unexpectedly and that one must *always* be on the alert was illustrated years later in Gorongosa when Ken was hurrying along a game path in dense riverine thicket. Running ahead of the game guard he was carrying the rifle himself and, atypically, he was careless because of his haste. The leaf litter of the floor deadened his footsteps and as he came around a bend in the path, there a short distance ahead of him he found three very surprised buffalo. Startled by his sudden appearance the buffalo leapt up and ran in the direction in which they were facing, which was towards Ken. There was no time to use the rifle and Ken swung himself up onto an overhead branch and pulled his legs right up as the three buffalo rushed under him. If they had not had their heads lowered to prevent the mass of small branches from scratching their eyes, their horns would have disemboweled the helpless Ken.

Another occasion brought a metre-long Gaboon viper to complicate working conditions in a swamp forest in Gorongosa. A local man who was working with Ken noticed the snake lying neatly camouflaged amongst the dead leaves of the forest floor. It was very difficult to see lying there so motionless, brown amongst brown, triangular head amongst triangular leaves, and body completely covered. Ken acknowledges with horror that he must have walked within paces of the quiet and sinister head. There was still work to be done in that area of the forest so the deadly poisonous animal was dispatched without much regret. The man who had discovered the snake told Ken that his tribe believed the Gaboon whistles for its food. Lying hidden in the leaves it calls like a bird to attract any feathered friends in the vicinity. If there is anything more curious than a cat it is a bird, and I can quite believe that a victim could in this way be lured right up to within striking range of the patient snake's head.

Leaving Ken to his data collecting and the black man to his vigilance I would enjoy lying flat on my tummy to observe the coming and going of animals in the grass or over the pale sands that are blackly speckled with carbon from innumerable yearly fires. To me sand-country is especially fascinating as the footprints of every beast, big or little, are left as signatures long after they have passed. Small cat footprints, hippo, hyaena, warthog, the long slim kangaroo prints of the springhare, the slither marks of snakes, and the thousand small criss-crosses from birds. Even lightweight black beetles blundering along leave impressions like tiny caterpillar tractors' trails. The small paired prints of the jumping rat or gerbil can also be seen, with now and then the marks of the little front paws. The gerbils dig shallow burrows in the sand which are quite a hazard to the unsuspecting walker as they may suddenly give way under one's weight.

I found another little tunnel digger one day by receiving a shower of sand in the eye whilst I was studying something on the ground. It was a small pale cricket not more than a centimetre in length. This little creature was digging a neat round tunnel and getting rid of the excavated sand by flicking it with broad comb-like appendages on its hind limbs. The spattering shower was falling a metre or more away on to the dry leaves. I dug the cricket out of its new house to have a better look. It was absolutely albino in colouring and the little 'rakes' or combs on its legs were perfectly formed; exquisite little built-in digging tools.

I was delighted one evening to hear the warning song of termites. In the Caprivi many pale clay termite castles or mounds line the edges of the floodplains and dambos. We were having a look at the dense thicket growing around the base of one of these termite mounds. Creepers wove a tight canopy and the floor was carpeted by that obnoxious lush grass that has sticky seeds which cling to any animal or human that passes. Walking up on to the side of the termite hill I was surprised to hear a faint, thin, rustling sound that grew and then faded into a whisper before I could locate its origin. Puzzled, I stood still; but it was gone. I moved a step forward and it started up again, a whispering movement or a moving whisper. Ken laughed to see how intrigued I was, and explained that it was the sound of millions of tiny termite heads tapping on their tunnel walls in warning to the rest of the nest that something was disturbing their castle.

Driving down to the southern boundary of the Strip we found a few patches of mopane woodland growing on the clay of old drainage lines. These mopane are tall and straight, making the gnarled and stunted trees of Etosha seem like shrubs. Eighteen to twenty metres high, they grow close together in a beautiful cool, green woodland. As in all mopane communities the undergrowth was sparse but we were surprised at the amount of birdlife here nevertheless. Crimson-breasted shrike, babblers and white helmet-shrikes were the first we saw. Walking a little way into the woodland we came to a small pan; from a tree near the edge three or four red-billed hoopoes rose up cackling in alarm, their handsome black and white plumage shining in the sun. We saw the spoor of leopard in the mud and the wind brought the cowstable smell of buffalo. The pale clay around the muddy pool of last season's rain water was completely bare of plant growth, trampled and moulded into pockmarks and craters of footprints. Most of the trees nearest the pan showed the more violent signature of elephant, torn and battered, many of them pushed over completely, lying blackened and rotting on the bare ground.

We dug a soil pit in the mopane woodland to see the composition of the subsurface layers and to take samples. While we were doing so small red heads peered at us from the trees and fluffy tails flicked agitatedly.

There was a surprising number of squirrel in the woodland. Then an Arnott's chat flashed before us, landing on a tree trunk with flirted tail and cocked head, brilliant in black and white. Later we saw the silver forms of white-breasted cuckoo shrikes glide between the trees and hornbills flap through the air.

Whilst we were in the Caprivi I became aware of a fascinating aspect of the bird inhabitants of the bush. Ken had delegated to me the task of making the bird checklist and notes. I had some previous knowledge of birds and Ken taught me to identify them from their calls alone. He also taught me how to attract them by sitting still and making a loud 'shisk shisk' noise. This approximates a bird's alarm call and the curious creatures come from far and wide to see what is causing the fuss. Like the Gaboon viper, you can attract the little creatures very close as long as you do not move at all. I have had flycatchers, robins, bulbuls, and shrikes within arm's distance of me, peering with their bright beads of eyes yet not seeing me. As many as ten species may gather, nervously flitting overhead before they decide there is nothing to be seen after all and they wander off.

In the Caprivi I learnt for the first time that particular birds occur only, or mainly, in particular plant covers or habitats. Walking through thorn veld almost anywhere in southern Africa you will see the yellowbill hornbill with his roguish, piratical, yellow eye or the tiny powder-blue waxbills, or hear the nasal piping of the pied barbet. These birds are not normally found in forest, woodland, or grassland, they are as characteristic of the thorn veld as the acacias themselves. Whereas in the dense shade of riverine woodland, you might glimpse the pink breast of a nerina trogon or hear the conversational chortles of the green pigeon as they feed in a fig tree; and in the grasslands you may see pipits, larks and long-claw fly up, though they are seldom seen elsewhere.

All birds do not of course adhere rigidly to the particular plant cover that suits them best, and their movement is often widespread and determined by the availability of food. However, it always amused me that in thorn country or thicket you could immediately *expect* to hear the complaining 'Gowaay' of the grey lourie or the plaintive lengthy lament of the emerald-spotted wood dove; and you missed them if you did not. In the Zimbabwean teak woodlands of the Strip you would listen for the call of the crested hornbill and at night the delightful repetitive 'Scronk' of the small, bark-and-lichen-coloured Scops owlet. Along the open river banks you would expect to see the white fronted bee-eater, whilst his brother the little bee-eater would be found in the open tree savannas, perching on low branches or bushes.

In the wooded areas of the Caprivi I noticed how at times bird parties would gather. Suddenly, and seemingly for no reason, the trees and bushes would be alive with small flutterings, chirpings and squabblings. Attracted by some commotion, or perhaps by a woodpecker calling his 'drumbeat' call (which sounds like a marble bouncing on a wooden floor and is made by the bird tapping a hollow log in a particular sequence), the birds come together in fluttering talkative groups, all feeding on their own particular foods. These parties move around for some time from one place to another until the birds gradually disperse again. Why exactly the parties form is a question long asked by ornithologists. A possible reason is that the excitement and movement of the group may disturb more insects than a bird feeding on its own. Fruit-eating birds will however also join a party, so perhaps one of the reasons for the habit is that they simply enjoy being together and this sociableness overrides the usual territorial rules of some species.

15

The Dreaded Tsetse

The Kwando River forms the eastern boundary of the Western Caprivi and from Bwabwata it was a major expedition to travel the sixty-odd kilometres to reach it. Our first trip was overland, driving along the dry grassed floor of a long drainage line. It took the whole day to get to our destination as we had to stop every hour or two to blow the grass seeds out of the radiator of the car where they collected and threatened to catch fire. As we neared the Kwando the blood-sucking tsetse fly made its appearance and was soon so prolific that despite the heat we had to drive with every window and vent closed.

Attracted to the bulk of the vehicle as they would be to a large animal, the flies crept in wherever possible and having once fed on us hung bloated and purple like grapes from the windscreen or windows. They were unbelievably numerous, which mystified us, seeing that there was so little game in the vicinity on which they could feed. Tsetse are shade-loving insects, they breed under bushes and trees and do not frequent open grasslands. They are however attracted to the shade of a vehicle or large animal. Their bites can be extremely painful (they left bruises on the soft parts of our arms and legs) and a large number of them can almost drive you out of your mind.

Later that day, on arriving at the track once again, we met a surveyor who was working on the opening of the boundary lines. Driving his truck he was unable to fend off the flies; by the time we saw him the stabbing agony and sticky persistence of the attackers had turned him into a stammering wreck. We gave him a bottle of insect repellent that we had found kept the flies at bay for a short while at least. The poor man poured the liquid into trembling hands and splashed it all over his face and into his eyes! The pain must have been tremendous but with tears and fresh water the repellent was eventually washed out and he continued hastily and red-eyed on his way out of the tsetse belt.

The Kwando in this area flows through a broad floodplain, whose northern reaches proved to be even more beautiful than the Okavango. Wide stretches of golden grassland flanked the river which itself was hidden behind thick riverine woodland. Dark islands of trees and Phoenix palms dotted the grasslands. Turning parallel to the river we pushed on southwards. We passed a few groups of impala, five kudu and one reedbuck. Travelling along the grasslands where we could, we were sometimes forced up on to the fairly steep slopes of the marginal floodplain woodlands, where tall stately knobthorn acacias were interspersed with clumps of thicket and grassed glades. We flushed a tiny pearl-spotted owl from his hiding place in one of the thickets and he settled again quite close to the car: a perfect creature not more than ten centimetres tall with clear, round yellow eyes and large grey flecks on a pale breast.

We stopped for a meal of rancid bread, cheese and oranges on a bank overlooking the river. Over our heads was a dead tree trunk, obviously the favourite perch of the fish eagle who landed on it with a rustle of feathers as if from a silken garment and looked down at us with a yellow imperious eye. The river was smooth and undisturbed; we had seen a group of hippo earlier but in this stretch there was none. There were no signs of crocodile either but we saw two smooth dark heads of otter bob up nearby.

That night we decided to return prematurely to our base camp at Bwabwata. Ken was worried that he would not be able to complete the collection of woodland analysis samples that he had begun at Bwabwata before fire spread through the now tinder-dry grass below the trees. So we turned back after sunset in order to reach Bwabwata that night and be able to start work early the next morning.

The freshly opened boundary line with the uninhabited wilds of Angola on our right stretched on endlessly before us, the headlights showing up the broken surface of the track and the ghosts of trees to each side. Suddenly through the darkness ahead of us we saw a light. It was so unexpected that at first we thought it must be the reflection from an animal's eye; but it was too distant and too yellow. Then the light started to flash at fairly regular intervals. It was eerie. We were in remote country hundreds of kilometres from any human habitation – apart from the small primitive settlement at Bwabwata which lay another twenty kilometres further on; and yet someone was flashing a light, sending some sort of message in fact, to us.

What was disturbing was that no one could have known we were there as we had not been due to return from the Kwando for several days yet. I wondered with dry mouth and thumping heart if the people ahead were not perhaps some of the armed insurgents who had lately begun crossing the Okavango River into Namibia. This was the very beginning of the SWAPO terrorist movement aimed at the territory. The SWAPO guerillas, based in Angola, were trained elsewhere in Africa, or in Russia. Before our arrival in the Caprivi a few of them had been apprehended in the Okavango area, but as far as we knew none had yet attempted coming through the Strip. Possibly this was a group of terrorists mistaking us for some of their comrades! Trusting that there was in fact another explanation we continued driving. There was no point in stopping as the light-flasher would know our position anyway.

The light kept flashing, on, off, on, off. It was as though we were hypnotised, moving painfully slowly towards it, unable to go any faster, unable to stop. At last we came upon it. A large truck stood beside the track, a camp was made and tents pitched. In the middle of the track, a powerful torch in his hands, stood the surveyor of the boundary-opening party – the man whom we had rescued from the tsetse. He had realized that it must be us travelling after dark and had thought that perhaps one of us was ill or that something was wrong and had signalled to show that he was there to give assistance if needed.

16

Marooned on a Floodplain Island

During our second trip to the Kwando boundary of the Strip the severe jolting that our truck had been subjected to began to tell now that we were at the furthest point from a garage and spares. As we bumped over the excruciating tracks the springs on the front left-hand side of the vehicle began to snap one by one. There was nothing we could do but carry on. Soon the whole set were through and we were stranded eighty kilometres from Bwabwata, the nearest village and hundreds of kilometres from the nearest garage. Our situation was not particularly serious however as the truck was equipped with a radio for this sort of emergency, and we were carrying enough provisions to last a week or ten days. Ken contacted Okaukuejo on the radio and they promised to send a mechanic and spares as soon as possible from Grootfontein, which at three hundred kilometres away was the nearest place where the spares would be available. The mechanic eventually reached us ten days later.

In order to make ourselves comfortable while waiting for the mechanic, we spent some time in locating the best possible camping site. With the aid of the air photos, which are necessary tools for Ken's work, and with his infallible eye for a good site, we found a snug thicket standing like an island in the grassland and overlooking a bend of the river and thick reedbeds. Being isolated from the main fly-infested bush this patch was free of tsetse, as the fly do not venture far out into the sunshine. It was also close to water for drinking, washing, and bathing. We carried no tent with us while in the Caprivi, as it was the dry season at that time, but the thick canopy of the thicket would protect us from any unseasonal shower or from wind. It was an ideal bush-house of the most primitive kind.

Ken made a rough clearing inside the thicket and we laid out our sleeping gear and food trunks. A small fire was built in the centre of the clearing and Johannes made a broom of a bundle of grass to sweep out the leaf litter and insects.

It had always been necessary for Ken's work that we travel with a third person. At this particular time Simon was not available and Johannes had made the Kwando trip with us. As a camping companion Johannes had been a mistake all along the line. He had accompanied us to the Caprivi as a cook and a general help for fetching water, washing pots and so on. As a cook however he was of no use and could be trusted with nothing more complicated than boiling water. Garlic salt in our morning porridge was what finally lost him this post. He had his dignity though, did poor Johannes, and he made great show of his usefulness at Bwabwata by hunting down rats in the supplies hut and beating them to death with as much noise and violence as possible. He wore a well-washed string bag that had once held oranges around his neck. This served very well as scarf, dishcloth and rat catcher.

But being on the Kwando and living like a primitive bushman did not suit the gentlemanly old Ovambo at all. He was lonely, and apart from that he thoroughly disapproved of this kind of existence and of all the 'empty' country around us. Coming from the settled cattle country of Ovamboland, he felt that these vast grass plains were all very well but completely wasted without any people and *beeste* to occupy them! There was very little for Johannes to do during those days of being marooned. He was no good at fishing, nor at setting traps for game birds, so he spent most of his time gathering firewood, boiling drinking water, sweeping the camp, sleeping, or slipping surreptitiously down to a hidden part of the river to bathe. On these bathing trips he often concealed a sawn-off gemsbok horn under his shirt and Ken explained much to my amusement that this was the original form of enema.

Despite the mournful Johannes, Ken and I settled down to enjoy our Swiss Family Robinson existence. Our food supply was adequate for more than a week, apart from sugar, which was almost finished. As I had honey and a tin or two of condensed milk that was certainly no problem. Powdered milk was also short but we could do without that too. The third thing that was running low was toilet paper, and I made a note to ask the mechanic to bring some with him. However Ken told me that the fragrant bush that we had always called 'black rhino food' could well be used as a substitute. The leaves are soft and delightfully scented; what more could one ask?

To supplement our food supply we thought we would catch fish. As there was no sharp bank near the camp, from which we could fish – the water seeped up through the grassland to within metres of our front door – Ken and Johannes built a little platform of logs out near a gap in the reeds. We had only to wade through water a little more than knee-deep before reaching the platform and from there could sit high and dry, and safe from crocodile, while we fished. The platform was made by lashing poles together with the wire that we very fortunately had amongst our equipment. It was a stocky, stable fishing platform and perfect for its purpose or for sitting in the sun and watching the bowing reed plumes, the sparkling water and the tiny fish swimming amongst the reed stalks in the clear amber water.

While the men were building the platform I made a saucepan bread in the battered handleless saucepan which turned out such a nice round tall loaf. I had enough flour for only three or four such loaves, but fortunately there were still packets of wholewheat biscuits in the food trunk. Then I began catching frogs and grasshoppers for bait, as we had not had much luck finding worms. Catching frogs was not so easy either. I would splash through mud and water for half an hour, stalking and springing upon alert little frogs who seemed fully aware of my intentions and regularly dived under the water to escape me. And when I did finally manage to grasp a slippery little body securely Ken would discover that this particular frog was one that he had not yet collected – and so into the collecting bottle it would go, and another frog had to be found for bait.

Our fishing never came to very much and Ken and I caught only two small fish. Johannes cut himself an enormous pole with which he attempted to fish, using a large lump of *putu* porridge on the hook as bait.

At night, as we lay on our camping mattress, the fire shut out all but a small circle of the night. Johannes lay recumbent on his bed of cut grass close enough to the fire to toast himself. A bare electric light bulb was strung from the acacia above us (this was fed by the car's battery and there was always a panic in the morning in case the radio wouldn't start because the battery was flat, so we had to leave the car engine running for an hour or so to recharge it). A wire three-legged pot-stand stood next to the fire holding a soot-blackened, ash-smeared saucepan. White towels and garments hung on surrounding bushes to discourage inquisitive or unwary hippo that might blunder into us during their nightly rambles. The rifle, broom, and my handbag stood propped up against the centre tree. The black food trunk was behind us and a pile of firewood loomed up on the other side of the fire.

Through the night the chorus of frogs and toads would grow noisier. Starting from a tinkling chorus, as of windbells, the variety of calls expanded and intermingled into confused waves of sound like radio

atmospherics. We heard no large animal sounds during those nights on the Kwando except a hyaena once, and in the early hours of morning a lion roared from far off. Drumbeats often came to us faintly but clearly from the villages of the Eastern Caprivi on the opposite bank of the wide river. A python once slithered past us through the dry undergrowth, unseen but identifiable by the length of the slithering. In the mornings coucal bubbled cascades of notes onto the tangy misty air and the wild voice of the fish eagle hailed the sun.

One morning we heard two fish eagle calling above us. As we watched they flew close to one another; and catching hold of each others' talons, they tumbled downward, somersaulting and twisting in the air. This was their courtship flight, what luck to have seen it! Once above the floodplain we saw a fish eagle whirling in a thermal with a flapping fish clutched in his talons. Was it a sadistic delight that led him to do this or was he allowing himself the double pleasure of having the pull of his anticipated meal in his strong claws while the wind surged under his wings?

My days were mostly taken up by writing in my diary and drawing. I would lie sunbathing on the fishing platform too, enjoying the river around me and the fat sounds of hippo on the far side of the reeds. One morning I saw a lilac-breasted roller doing aerobatics. It tumbled and twisted through the air, dropping like a leaf and flashing turquoise, as bright as a sequin. A black crake dabbled in the water at the foot of the reeds, almost invisible in the strong shadows, and ripples fanned out glinting behind two toy-like dwarf geese which were swimming silently over the pearl sheen of the water. Catching sight of me the geese rose and with piping whistles circled and landed again – heads up and wings beating downwards – a little way off. The black crake, which was now completely invisible, started up a duet with its mate; a deep churring by one and a high peeping by the other sung in unison, an unusual combination of sound, pleasing and comical! Then a fearful crashing suddenly started in the flooded reeds and became interspersed with sharp squeaks. I could not see what was making the noise but suspected that it might be otter fighting or mating. We had been surprised by the number of otter in the Kwando. Possibly the scarcity of crocodile and the relative lack of disturbance by man have allowed them not only to breed, but to become less shy in these reaches of the river.

Out on the floodplain near to our camp was a small herd of lechwe, a remnant from a far greater population. It was sad to think that the once vast herds of these graceful red buck had been reduced to the fourteen animals that we now saw.

The lechwe is, even more than the waterbuck, the antelope that has evolved to make use of the seasonally-inundated floodplain systems of Africa. It lives in the marshy sodden grasslands, sometimes grazing with its muzzle submerged in the water, and fleeing when in danger, not to bush or reed cover, but deeper into the water. It is this habit that has made it so susceptible to predation by man as it is easily speared or shot from canoes.

Tan-red in colour with large black eyes and sweeping white throats, the lechwe is particularly characterized by its slightly shaggy coat and high rump. The males have long lyre-shaped horns. The name comes from their call which is a whistling 'Lestwee'. The alarm snort is a harsh and unexpected raspberry.

The Kwando lechwe were not particularly worried by our presence even though we were on foot. We could creep up behind cover of a termite hill to within twenty paces of them and watch them at leisure for twenty to thirty minutes as they comfortably grazed, the wide golden plains dotted with palm thickets spreading out behind them.

One afternoon soon after midday we heard a bounding through the water on the far side of our bend in the river. Going up to our termite hill lookout we could see over the reeds to where a lechwe was pronking through the shallows in a distracted manner, shaking his head and kicking his heels. For over half an hour we watched the poor creature try to rid himself of the numerous tsetse fly which we think must have been worrying him. He was turning his head from side to side to lick his flanks and to rub his chin along his back. He wandered around in small circles, sometimes splashing water on to his back with his muzzle and trying to bite at the flies. He lay down for a short while, whether it was in the shallows or on dry land we could not see, and then eventually becoming calmer he wandered off into the reeds. Probably he had approached too close to a fly-infested thicket and attracted the parasite which does not normally like to be out in the bright sunlight. Presumably the lechwe's tolerance threshold must be very much lower than impala, for impala live in the same habitat as the tsetse and do not seem to be too worried by the fly.

17

Encounter with a Family of Elephant

Exploring the Kwando area on foot, we would walk for hours on end through thornbush and grassland, the sweat running in continuous and sticky streams down our bodies. I would walk behind Ken and wave a handkerchief in the vain attempt to keep the swarms of tsetse off his back, as for some reason they vastly preferred him to me. Ken carried the rifle over one shoulder and his note pad, often with one or two air photos clipped on to it from which he could detect any interesting changes in vegetation or bend in the river which called for a visit. I carried a sketch book and the binoculars slung around my neck on a long piece of plaited dish cloth, as the leather thong had worn through some weeks earlier. We seldom carried food or drink but would return to camp in the late afternoon to heavenly huge and steaming mugs of lemon tea. Bottles of lemon squash or bags of fresh lemons were always a necessary part of our bush equipment as lemon tea is the most refreshing and reviving drink we have found.

One midday we happened to be walking along the boundary track, keeping as much as possible in the sun to avoid the tsetse. The birds were resting and quiet, as they always were during the hottest hours of the day, and the tall acacias and silver Terminalias dangled limp, lifeless leaves. Fat clouds occasionally shut off the sunlight for intervals of coolness, and then the rays would burn through again, drenching the bush and white sand in light and us in sweat. Walking quietly we came across a small herd of impala which bolted as soon as they saw us, and further on two warthog were wallowing in a mudhole. They too rushed off, their round fat buttocks glistening with patches of wet mud and their tails erect. The sand of the track showed spoor of a variety of animals from hippo to genet cat and hyaena, but apart from our own not one of a human.

Around a bend just where the track ran beside a small waterhole Ken stopped abruptly. 'There are elephant ahead,' he said. I could neither see nor hear a trace of the big animals but somehow Ken had sensed them. We crouched down alongside the track and waited. A few seconds later an elephant cow walked on to the track some thirty paces ahead of us. She was followed by another cow and a half-grown calf. They walked down to the water at the edge of the track and began to drink.

Whispering, Ken told me that we should remain crouched down so that we didn't look like humans, and make our way slowly to the other side of the track where we might slip away upwind of the elephant. However before we could move the calf finished his drink, and turning in our direction ambled slowly forward. Suddenly he caught sight of us. Immediately his expression grew alert and he tested the air with the tip of his trunk. I doubt if he could have scented us as the wind was not in his favour. But sure in his mind that there was danger he lightly and quickly touched his mother on her flank with the tip of her trunk. In a second all three elephants wheeled and melted back into the bush the way they had come. The warning was given and reacted to so swiftly and silently that Ken and I could hardly believe it. With hammering heart and dry mouth I followed Ken off in the opposite direction!

It is well known that young elephant and young rhino are more observant than their elders. An old friend of ours, Jim Feely, who has worked for most of his life in the Zululand bush and in the Luangua valley of Zambia, claims that the adults become conditioned to sights around them and lose their curiosity. Anything that doesn't move goes unnoticed by them, but the youngsters with their more agile and enquiring minds will immediately notice anything that is unusual whether it moves or not. This sharp-eyed little elephant had definitely seen us, immobile as we were, the minute he looked in our direction.

During another of our walks we saw a poacher camp strewn with the bones of hippo. An elephant skeleton, without the tusks, lay bleached and ash dry in the thorn veld some way from the camp. From the opposite bank of the river one morning we heard the heavy report of a big rifle. Apart from the boundary surveyor we had not seen another human being in the Kwando; but obviously they were there from time to time. The shortage of crocodile and hippo bore testament to heavy shooting of these populations, not to mention the lechwe which usually occur in such large herds and yet on these floodplains were reduced to so few.

After a week our food supply was beginning to run dangerously low. Because of the disheartening lack of game in the area Ken was not keen to shoot for the pot although we had been given permission to do so. Johannes however did not echo our sentiments and his complaints about the lack of meat caused Ken to attempt to shoot a large old warthog, one of the few we had seen in the Caprivi. The hog was partly obscured by shrubs so that Ken stepped back to take better aim. In so doing he tripped over a dead branch and crashed backwards into its thorny clutches. Johannes and I split our sides with laughter, and whilst Ken sheepishly extricated himself, the surprised old hog trotted nearer to see what was going on. Of course there was no second attempt on his life! Warthog, I later heard, can be particularly aggressive and once roused have very little fear. Ken told me how he had seen a male hog in Moremi, Botswana, rout a lion, going at him like a miniature tank and chasing him off.

Late on the afternoon of our tenth day on the Kwando the mechanic finally arrived. With him he had his wife and two small children – little girls of about four and two. We were amazed that they had brought their children to this tsetse-infested area, especially as we knew that there was a danger of contracting the fatal sleeping sickness that the tsetse carries. Apart from this there was a risk of catching bilharzia from the water and malaria from the mosquitoes. However the Moolmans appeared oblivious to all these disadvantages and were determined to enjoy their stay. They unpacked a case of beers, a bottle of brandy and fishing gear. They also brought a mutton rib which we grilled that night over the coals. It was the first fresh meat we had eaten for a month and it tasted like butter on our delighted tongues.

Once the vehicle was repaired we left ahead of the Moolmans and hotfooted it out of the Caprivi. Soon after our return to Etosha we went to Windhoek and had medical tests for bilharzia and sleeping sickness. Fortunately we had picked up neither; but I was left with a legacy from our bush trip. Somewhere under a sagging thatch hut roof or starry sky I had conceived the son who was to be born to us at the end of that year.

Analyses of the Caprivi soils indicated as Ken had suspected that the Western Strip would be unsuitable for agricultural settlement; yet it was ideal for a variety of wildlife populations. He drew up a report in which he recommended that the Strip should remain in its natural state, and that the hunter-gatherer hottentot groups should continue to live there as part of the ecological whole. Decisions on the future of the Strip were shelved, however, when the Caprivi and the Okavango region were overrun with terrorists during the following year; the Strip then became a purely military zone, occupied by South African troops.

Part Two
MOÇAMBIQUE

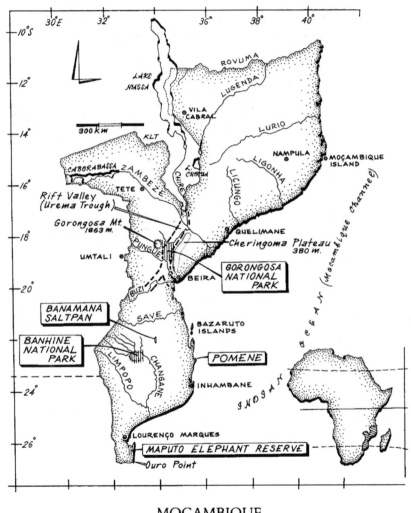

MOÇAMBIQUE

18

Heading East

In 1967 during October, that dreadful 'suicide month' of Namibia, when everything is bone dry and baking hot, we traveled down to Windhoek expecting our first child to arrive in six or seven days. Three weeks later we were still waiting, staying with friends, our tempers and patience wearing thin. Ken took up duties at the Head Office at this time and he endured the eight-to-five city routine with less and less good humor every day. He hated having to wear the regulation uniform and, worst of all, socks with his shoes; he resented office life and its desk-bound bureaucrats. Eventually however, early in November, Allan was born and we were able to return to Etosha.

Some months later Ken received a letter from the Fauna and Flora department of the Portuguese government inviting him to do ecological studies of the Gorongosa National Park in Moçambique. The prospect thrilled us. We had been extremely happy in Etosha but the temptation to break new ground and to experience life in a new country proved to be overwhelming and Ken accepted the invitation with little hesitation. During our last few months in Etosha we began to learn the Portuguese language and found it a happy experience to roll our tongues around the new, soft-sounding words.

In the middle of 1968 our luggage was shipped from Walvis Bay all the way around the coast of southern Africa to Lourenço Marques (now Maputo), the capital of Moçambique, and we flew in with Allan and his meager baggage of nappies and vests which were all the clothing he had needed in Etosha.

A taxi driver introduced us to the casual verve of Latin drivers in a breakneck journey from the airport through the reed hut slums of the city to the hotel where we were to spend the night. Moçambique was like a new world to us: we found the Latin-African atmosphere and way of life immediately attractive, and the generous warmth and old-world courtesy of the people endearing.

Once Ken's papers were in order we embarked on the long, long drive from the capital up to Gorongosa. The journey lasted three exhausting days of sweltering heat, dust, and bad roads. Fortunately I was breast feeding the baby and so did not have to worry too much about the lack of hygiene in the small candle-lit, cockroach infested rooms of the *pensões* at which we spent the two nights on the road. We drove in convoy, with a game ranger from Gorongosa, Mendes, in the lorry containing our goods and us in Ken's new official green Land-Rover. The tar road lasted all of one day and then we reached the rutted gravel and sand roads. Along the coast plantations of coconut palms lined the road -graceful palms with feathery plumes that rattled in the wind and stuck together like wet eyelashes in the rain. The solid stands of palms bent and swayed in the wind, alive with greens, yellows, and tans. The tribal people who tend the plantations build small quaint huts of plaited palm frond between the slender trunks and climb the palms by means of notches to gather the nuts.

The halfway point of this seemingly endless journey northwards is marked by the Save River. A new bridge spans the Save, but at that stage it was incomplete and cars and lorries struggled through the sand ford as all traffic has done since man's first journey up and down Moçambique. A typical rural trading store stood before the bridge. On the dusty veranda sat several lethargic locals tolerating the flies and the heat, and a mongrel

scratching at its mangy pelt. Mendes ordered bread rolls with piri-piri sardines and coffee for lunch. Any little store or village in Moçambique had at that time excellent strong black coffee to offer and the inevitable home-baked floury breads, fresh and hard-crusted. These cut in half with a few tinned piri-piri sardines sandwiched in between is a meal equal to none for a hungry traveller—especially together with the rich black coffee!

By our sides a black urchin appeared with a living red scrap in his hands. My heart gave a lurch as I saw that it was a baby red duiker – a small forest antelope which is of a deep burnished copper colour. The boy wanted to sell it, but he had approached the wrong people. Mendes leapt at once on to his official Game Department high horse and, gesticulating wildly, berated the little scoundrel at great length. The boy received nothing for his pains but I got the duiker. I was apprehensive: it was a very small baby, and we had another day and a night to travel before we could get the little wild creature comfortable and quiet. She was exquisite; calm and resigned, with huge liquid black eyes and a tiny wet rubbery nose. She accepted milk out of an eye dropper almost immediately and lay quietly in a straw-lined box for the whole terrifyingly bumpy journey. But when we eventually arrived in Gorongosa the rigours of the journey caught up with her and she died in convulsions on our first night there.

After the Save River bridge we met our first Moçambique tsetse fly. Fortunately they were not numerous and if any stung small plump Allan, as he lay in only a nappy on an improvised cot in the back of the Rover or bounced on my lap, he did not squeal. The country became very wild and very arid. This was Moçambique's 'thirstland', and yet it was quite different from the great Namibian 'thirstland' from which we had just come. Trees were bigger here, giant purple baobab towered over the road, the bush was denser, and the air had a thickness of some humidity unlike the sharp crackling aridity of Namibia. There was not much game to be seen along the road although it was good big game habitat with glades of grasslands and clumps of acacias. Human habitations became few and far between, and the ones we did see – often huddled around a small mission station – made us realize that boreholes to supply water must be essential to human life in this area.

At sunset on the following day, driving once again through moist savannas as the arid zone had been left far behind, we eventually arrived at Vila Machado, where the road to Gorongosa branches off from the main road between Umtali and Beira. It was dark by the time we reached the Pungue River which forms part of the southern boundary of the park and can be crossed by a floating bridge during the dry season. Half an hour later the winding narrow road took us through the Gorongosa gate. Here a line of short, deformed telephone poles flanked the track. Cut roughly from local trees, some were sprouting vigorous green leaves at the top, while others were knocked awry by elephant. Drunkenly the poles and their sagging wires led us on through a second gate and into a grove of mango trees whitewashed around their bases. This was Chitengo, only rest camp of the park, and our home for the next four and a half years.

19

The Living Plains of Gorongosa

Gorongosa, named after the mountain that overlooks it, and in fact nourishes it with life-giving annual floods, and which in turn took its name from the first chief who settled in the area, lies across the tail-end of the Great Rift Valley of East Africa. The Rift, in this area named the Urema Trough or Moçambique Rift, has here flattened out considerably, its low walls sloping and carved out by streams. The valley is thirty-five to forty kilometres broad in the Gorongosa area and it runs further south-east and into the sea at the ancient Arab seaport of Sofala. Gorongosa Mountain is not part of the Rift wall but lies behind it to the west and is an isolated granite block left after the erosion of a previous land surface. Solid and long, the mountain reaches 1868 metres at its highest peak. It forms a barrier, in an otherwise low landscape, to the moist sea air blowing inland during the day. The air rises at the massif to form dense white clouds which pour their load of rain down each afternoon of the wet season on to the spongy grasslands and the dripping rain forests of the summit and slopes.

Gorongosa, which is immensely rich in a variety of large animals, was proclaimed a game reserve by the Portuguese Government in 1921 and in 1960 was made a National Park. Some thirty to sixty kilometres in size, the park lies one hundred and twenty kilometres from Beira and just off the main route from this seaport to the interior and Zimbabwe; so it must have been seen by the very first explorers in the territory. Traders and ivory hunters active in East Africa from as far back as before the time of Christ must have repeatedly passed through or hunted on the Gorongosa floodplains. But this unique natural system, linked to the Marromeu swamps of the Zambesi delta in the north, is so rich and productive, and such a paradise for migrating elephant, wildebeest and buffalo, that despite man's depredations on the animal populations he has in fact not seriously threatened their viability.

Ken's first task in Moçambique was to determine the ecological boundaries of the Gorongosa system and to recommend where the borders of the park should run so as to enclose as complete and independent a natural system as possible. This is something that has very seldom been achieved in wilderness areas or national parks in Africa. Usually the intricate order within a protected area is threatened by pollution, overcrowding or bad land management over its borders, owing to lack of foresight and planning at the time of the border demarcation. Ken had realized from studying maps of the area even before we arrived in Gorongosa that the isolated mountain massif was probably the main water catchment area for the park, its floodplains and most of the surrounding ground, and that it was essential to protect this catchment in order to assure the health and variety of the park system as well as the surrounding human communities. Later he was to draw up proposals indicating how the park boundaries should be modified to include the mountain and how the whole area could be planned, in the simplest possible manner, for tourist viewing, for research and education, for wilderness areas, and for the cropping of game as a source of protein for the surrounding tribal people.

The amazing abundance and variety of animal life in Gorongosa is due to the huge floodplains which become shallowly inundated during the wet season. Thousands of hippo occupy this water; in the dry season they become restricted to the Urema Lake and River in the centre of the plains. The hippo fertilize the water with their droppings, and this, combined with the fact that the flooding prevents grazing for three to four months each year, makes the grasslands, once the flooding has subsided, extremely rich. Thousands upon thousands of head of game – oribi, waterbuck, zebra, wildebeest, impala, reedbuck, eland, warthog, buffalo and elephant – utilize these pastures whilst they are exposed and green. Once they have dried out most of the animals seek the numerous *vleis* or depressions scattered through the savanna and the lowest parts of the floodplains where the soil moisture has not all vanished and the grass is still green.

The birth of each yearly flood, which starts in about December and continues until February or March, takes place on the Gorongosa

Mountain. Here the rainfall is more than two thousand millimeters a year as compared with eight hundred millimeters a year on the Rift floor. The grassed summits and forested slopes of the mountain absorb this rain and send it gushing down its flanks in numerous clear streams. Three of the major rivulets run throughout the year into the Urema Lake and in the rainy season cause it to swell. The bottom, southern, end of the lake is restricted, as Ken soon detected from an aerial survey, by the flooding of a small stream off the sandy eastern flank of the Rift, the Cheringoma Plateau. As this stream gushes down to meet the Urema at the bottom end of the lake the silt and debris it brings with it fan out into the Urema, blocking the flow of the slowly moving river, and building up the waters of the lake across the vast flat plains behind.

Failure of the Cheringoma stream to flood, or removal of its alluvial fan by mechanical means, would open up the restriction of the Urema and the waters of the lake would run through instead of damming up. The flood-plain soils would dry out almost permanently, and acacia trees and palms would steadily encroach on land that used to be too waterlogged for them. After ten to fifteen years a savanna (tree and grass) system very much less rich and productive in animal life than the floodplain grasslands would have replaced them. Under present conditions the flooding is low some years but high enough in others for the standing waters to waterlog and drown the acacia and palm seedlings that are constantly invading wherever they can.

During our second summer in Gorongosa there was an exceptional flood. The lake's waters crept up under the tall fever tree woodlands peripheral to the plains, and the roads were submerged up to half a

metre. Ploughing through this in the Rover one day Ken nearly ran over a young crocodile swimming across the road!

One of my most vivid memories of the flooding season is of the herds of impala and their young which congregate in the woodlands above the flooding level. They spread out under the golden light of the fever tree woodland, glowing and flickering like flames. The hide of each animal shivers continuously and their white tails flash because of swarms of small black flies, commonly called wildebeest flies, that surround them. The flies used to be so bad at this time of the year that we could not stop the vehicle for a minute without being covered by them, having them in our ears, eyes and nostrils, which made drawing, writing or photography impossible.

Thousands of water birds arrive on the plains during the flooding to take advantage of the rich shallow waters. Egret, ibis, spoonbills, herons and divers nest in the tall *Acacia albida* (called winterthorns because they bear leaves in winter and shed them in summer) that hang over the water. The ancient, sleazy-looking Marabou stork in his funereal dress waits in the shallows under the trees for fledglings that fall out of the twig platforms above or for fish dropped by the parents during feeding. Crocodile also gather under the nesting trees to pick up the dropped food and to feed on fish attracted to the water enriched by birds' dung. A colony of pink pelican nest further back from the water in a clump of tall borassus palms. The weight of the birds and nests has disarranged and flattened the fan fronds and the graceful trees look like old and well-used prostitutes, maintaining a feminine charm but with hair here matted and there balding. The huge pelican chicks crouch in their insecure nests bellowing and mooing like calves, while the heavy bodies of the adults glide down on long-pinioned wings bringing more fish for the ever-hungry and gaping pink bills.

The African skimmer, a bird rarely seen in other areas, nested on islands in the lake. On a small bare island one summer we saw a colony of eight pairs that had made their nests in hollows in the ground. On the ground these short-legged birds look ungainly and heavy with their soot black backs and long thick crimson bills. But in the air their white bellies and underwings swoop with perfect aerodynamic grace as they skim the lake with elongated lower bills, and shear through the surface of the water like scissors through silk, fishing for algae and plankton.

Numerous waders nest in the dried mud above the edge of the water. The long sinuous shape of the leguaan, a giant lizard, slides cautiously around, black forked-tongue flickering as he searches for eggs or fledglings. Black and white blacksmith-plovers dive and flutter above his head, chinking strident abuse.

The floodplains are almost unbelievably rich in birds at this time. Pratincoles drift in clouds over the lake, their bellies shining silver in the sun, like shoals of tiny fish in the blue wave of the sky. Crested-crane adorn the grasslands, up to a hundred in a flock rising in front of us as we approach. Their melancholy trumpeting, 'kaaoooo kaaoooo', carries far and poignantly over the plains. Woolly-necked stork in pink breeding dress fish the small pans along with pairs of gaunt clown-clothed saddle bill stork. Pairs of the tall blue-grey, wattled crane, the biggest and the most elegant of the cranes, stride through the fever tree woodlands or perform measured courtship dances out on the heat-hazed plains.

Later in the year when the waters have retreated, the green floodplains have slowly dried out, and the short grasses are eventually brown, there are fewer birds; although some remain around the edges of the diminished lake and on pans that hold water. White pelican still float across the water, dipping and striking in unison in the characteristic concerted fish drives which always remind me of an earnest and rhythmical ballet – the white ruffled bodies of the dancers dipping as if to an elegant melody into the calm brightness of their own reflections. The fish eagle still halloos from dead trees and ponderously flies over the water in search of food or some other bird that he can rob of his catch of fish. But the great flocks are mostly gone, dispersed to far-lying pans and mud banks or migrated to the northern summer. Similarly, the game has moved from the plains into the savannas and woodlands or to distant, still marshy areas. Lone territorial wildebeest bulls may be left pawing up their stamping grounds and surveying the empty sere plains, the shimmering mirages and distant groups of waterbuck. Hippo lumbering out at night or on dull days to feed must wander further and further afield to find grazing for their lawnmower mouths and sometimes, despite their enormous size and strength, they fall prey to prides of lion.

And so the yearly cycle swings around – a spiral really, rather than a cycle, as the conditions are never exactly the same from year to year. Each summer there are a few new rain pans, new mud banks, new dongas, new plant invasions springing up where none was previously. Each winter there are new overgrazed areas, or undergrazed areas, new hippo paths, and channels, and kilometres upon kilometres of freshly burnt pastures. And for four and a half spirals we were in Gorongosa, soaking it up, recording what we could and being part of the plains, the hills, and the mountain.

20

Snake, Snails and Elephant

I have many vivid memories of Chitengo, the camp at Gorongosa, and the years we lived there; but all of them float in a basic remembrance of heavy heat and enervating humidity, like vegetables in a thick soup. The climate was extremely uncomfortable at times and annoying in that it was so unconducive to any kind of human activity, and so highly productive of insects, bacteria, and fungi all ready to attack the energy-sapped bodies of ourselves and the children. However there were many things that made up for the discomfort and for the numerous bouts of ill-health that we suffered. The very atmosphere of the place did much to displace any discontent I may have felt. The charm and odour of the exuberantly growing vegetation; the number of grey speckled dwarf gecko and other small animals about the house; the pale shafts of rain falling straight out of the sky in sullen monotony, dripping off the thatch and spreading in sheets before the front door – to be replaced the next morning by tiny castles and towers put up from the wet earth by termites for the launching of their flying forms. The 'breeep breeep' of the rain frog calling from the children's sandpit into which he had dug himself a burrow with his spade-like back feet, and the explosions of baby frogs soon after the rain; the green and gold of Gorongosa during the late mild winter when the palms and evergreen trees remain green whilst deciduous trees scatter gold leaves and fever trees bloom in strongly scented masses of yellow as bright as their trunks; the far, flat floodplains melting into mirages. All these and many other things made me forgive the Rift Valley its long humid summer months and clouds of savagely whining, malarial mosquitoes clustered at the gauze at night.

Snakes too stand out large and clear in my memory of Chitengo. This is mostly because the children were small and played outside so much that I often worried about them being bitten. During the hot dry months before the rain snakes were extremely numerous around Chitengo. During one October I recall having seen or killed fifteen night adders in our small garden and two *skaap-stekers* (a back-fanged and not too dangerous variety) in the house. One night adder, fortunately engorged with a recently swallowed frog, was very nearly sat upon by Tojo, Allan's companion and son of Carlos and Noemia Sarraiva, the tourist officers from the camp. Pedro, a twelve-year-old black boy whom I hired to keep Allan out of trouble, kept a strict eye on the little ones but slipped up once or twice in this demanding task. Once, while Pedro was missing for a short while, Allan found a red-lipped herald and did not hesitate in picking it up. This small snake is also back-fanged and so is not particularly dangerous to an adult, but one cannot be sure how an infant would react to its bite. Fortunately Ken happened to be passing just at that moment; he rapidly dispatched the snake and dealt out a beating to his son with the rolled scientific journal that he had in his hand. Poor Pedro was himself bitten one dusk near the garden tap. The snake, probably a *skaap-steker*, caught him on the big toe; we managed to inject him with serum fairly promptly so that he recovered after only one day of swelling and pain.

High up under the eaves of our house, beige and brown *Achatina* snails used to hibernate. With the onset of the rains they would slide gently down the walls, leaving slime trails up to ten centimetres wide. Emerging mostly at night these beautifully striped giant snails would silently graze on the lush grass and then return to the shelter of the house or trees during the day. A group of four *Achatina* once clustered under our bathroom window in the shade of a pawpaw tree. They left four round, slightly muddy impressions which at first sight gave me a thrill of horror as the group looked for all the world like the big pugmark of a lion that had jumped up against the wall to peer into our bathroom window.

Against the mosquito-netting screen of this same window we often saw a pair of the little grey and black speckled dwarf gecko. They had taken up residence there, as had a pair of their kind in almost every window of the house. These little lizards with pink suckered toes and large black eyes would wax fat on the scores of insects that trapped themselves against the screen. I had to be constantly on my guard against

crushing their fragile little bodies as I closed a window, but for all my care this did occasionally and tragically happen. The female gecko in the bathroom window appeared to be more than usually fertile. There was seldom a time when the oval shape of an egg could not be seen in her slightly pink translucent belly as she hung on the screen with the bright daylight behind her. Cold-blooded as they are, these little geckos are very passionate and sensual lovers. A mating pair would cling belly to belly for hours with their sinuous tails weaving in ecstasy around them.

We often had dinner beside an open fire at the back of the house. Over a bed of mopane coals we would grill meat if it was available, or seafoods, fish, prawns or squid bought in Beira. With the astringent red '*verde*' wines and hard-crusted Portuguese bread these were meals to be remembered. One still summer's evening an *Achatina* with striped shell gleaming dully in the firelight crept up on to a breadboard and discovered a splash of wine that I had spilt there. I heard a slight rasping noise beside me and there was the snail licking up the wine. When he had finished I dipped my finger into my glass and held it out to him. Without any hesitation the giant mollusc started licking my finger with his flat sandpaper-like tongue. Maliciously Ken and I fed him more and more wine until the soft slimy body drooped slackly from his shell when I picked him up and his stalked eyes and antennae swiveled erratically. After a while I put him down in a safe place to sleep off his intoxication.

Behind the house Ken arranged for two bungalows to be built of reed and thatch. One was a guest hut and the other, hexagonal in shape and with gauze windows all around, was my studio. It was one of the nicest places to paint, with plenty of light, air and space. Dust was a problem: it came sifting through the gauze and raining down from the thatch where termites and wood borers were constantly at work with an incessant soft rustling; but otherwise it was an ideal studio, where I could be alone and as undis-

turbed as a mother of young children can possibly be. I did have some sort of company in my hut. A fat shiny skink declared its window ledges his territory, ideal for basking in the sun and catching insects trapped inside the gauze. Under the ledge where this lizard slithered on his daily patrol was a hole in the reeds that housed an enormous baboon spider. I used to see him only at night when his black eyes glittered in the light that I was working by as he watched and waited for an opportunity to come out.

The mango and cashew nut trees that grew in the garden used to be frequented by fruit bats at night. Making their twanging, bicycle-pump squeak they would gorge themselves on the fruit and leave a scattering of dung and spat-out fibres under the trees where we had our breakfast in the morning. Smaller insectivorous bats made their homes under the thatch. The layers of their droppings used to pile up, melt during the rains and pour down the outer walls of the house leaving dark brown, strong-smelling stains. This smell is part of the atmosphere of every rural village in Moçambique!

A porcupine often bulldozed his way into the garden. We would hear him rattling about outside our porch, muttering in true porcupine fashion to himself and munching the juicy mangoes. Ken encountered a pair of these imperturbable creatures as he walked one night to the wind vane near the air strip. They were startled by his sudden appearance and one flicked its tail around rapidly, sending a spray of loose quills in Ken's direction – illustrating the origin of the story about the porcupine being able to 'shoot' quills at its enemy.

During the day vervet monkeys used to raid the mango trees, much to Allan's delight; and when he disturbed them each would lope off across the ground on three legs clutching a fruit in one hand and throwing cheeky glances over its shoulder. These same monkeys used to annoy Ken by eating the soft butter-yellow petals of the ginger plants that he had planted around his laboratory. The delicate flowers had no sooner opened than the monkeys would be upon them, leaving only a stripped and pungent stalk.

The aeroplane landing strip adjoining the camp was often used by wildebeest and impala, buffalo, or elephant as the mowed grass would shoot green and vigorous when other grazing was brown. Planes coming in to land to bring visitors to the park would as a matter of course buzz the strip to chase off the animals before landing.

One bright autumn morning after the mist had lifted off the airstrip José Tello, then Chief Game Warden of Gorongosa, came to our house yelling for Ken. When I offered José a cup of coffee he laughed. 'No, thank you.'

'I've had my *café*. I want to introduce Ken to two elephant.' Two young but mature bull elephant had wandered on to the airstrip and were pulling at the long grass that grew at its edges. They had in fact moved up very close to the camp gates by the time José saw them.

He had often told Ken that he was able to get very close to mild-tempered elephants, and that he turned them aside, if they did charge, by throwing out his arms and shouting at them. This brought back memories of Etosha and Pieter Stark's stories of creeping up behind resting elephant and pulling hairs out of their tails. I did not believe them at the time but I now think they were probably true!

José had recognized the two individuals on the airstrip and knew them to be placid beasts without any anxieties concerning the human race. Ken asked if I would like to come along: and suddenly that bubble of the joy of adventure that much of the time lies semi, or completely, submerged welled up in me and burst, despite my year-old son clutching at my ankles. I handed Allan to Pedro, and we set out. As we walked slowly through the airstrip gates towards the elephant I lagged behind the men and several times thought of turning back. But faith in Ken's judgment, if not in José's, reassured me, as I have never yet known Ken to take uncalculated risks, especially when his life is involved. So I kept on and hoped step after step that the men would now think we were close enough and stop.

As the distance between us shortened the elephant began to get restless; they fidgeted, and twiddled their trunks. One of them turned his back to us but continued to watch us out of the corner of his eye. At about fifty paces or less from the pair José stopped. I fluttered to a standstill a little way behind hoping that the elephant could not smell my fear. I could smell them: a warm musky smell, unlike the sharp acid scent given off by frightened elephant, and I could hear the loud slow swish of their ears. Then after a short while José and Ken slowly turned around and sauntered away, with me scurrying ahead breathing a long sigh of relief.

21

A Casa Maluca

A Portuguese artist visiting Chitengo once remarked with amusement that we lived in a *casa maluca*, a mad-looking house. I was quite hurt; but then I looked again at our small dwelling, squashed between the two barn-like porches we had added, the whole thing topped off with a sagging, blackened thatch reeking of bat dung, and I saw what he meant. Perhaps it was a *casa maluca*—but it served us well.

The house had been built as single quarters for two rangers and consisted originally of two small rondavel bedrooms with a living-room, bathroom and kitchen built between them. Tiny windows, set high in the walls, let in little light and even less fresh air. The sleepless, sweat-soaked nights that taxed us so badly during our first summer at Chitengo prompted Ken to have the two sleeping porches built on to the eastern and western sides of the house in readiness for the second summer. Then the cool air from the hinterland flowed in at night through the screening of the western porch, through the house, and out again at the other side, providing excellent natural air conditioning.

At night as we lay in our porch, the sounds, scents, and feeling of the dark tropical night were all around us. The leaves of the big mango tree spreading above the thatched roof whispered, fruit bats twanged, far-away drums throbbed, a hyena or lion might call, and sometimes from near the river came the long sweet soulful whistle of a water dikkop. During summer the perfume of mango or cashew nut blossoms or the heady ripe smell of fallen and fermenting fruit would drift around us.

In the house I had a helper whose name was Antonio. He was tall and skinny with big feet and big knees. Antonio must have felt he had come down in the world by working for us, as he had once worked in the house of the *Administradore* in Vila Paiva. He was very scornful of my slapdash housekeeping methods and our lack of silver and carpets. But despite his disapproving air and occasional bouts of drunkenness I got on fairly well with him. There was a lot of work to be done in the house even though it was small. We waged a constant war against cockroaches, so big and hungry that they would chew the plastic covering from electric wires; and mould, that would creep over shoes and books if cupboards were not aerated. Antonio would wash the clothes and each article would have to be ironed because of a parasite fly which lays its eggs on damp clothing. If not killed by a hot iron the larva of this fly burrows into human flesh, creating a large itchy swelling. Because we had no electricity during the day at Chitengo—the small generator worked only half of the night as in Okuakuejo—Antonio used a primitive ember iron to press the clothes. This had a cavity which had to be filled with red-hot embers from the fire, a time-consuming and messy business.

Antonio and I did not get on so well in our attempts to cultivate a vegetable garden. We each tended to blame the other for the failure of this particular venture, which was successful only in producing quantities of small red chillies which in fact we had not planted. Bushbuck and porcupine helped in the general deterioration of the vegetables, as well as nibbling the indigenous trees and shrubs which Ken had planted. The bushbuck would leap into the garden at night over the fence, which invariably made a jangling sound, and Ken would go bounding from our sleeping porch, stark naked and swearing violently in both English and Portuguese, and sometimes Zulu, to chase them away.

Looking back on those years in Gorongosa I often wonder how on earth we ever had enough to eat. The bulk of the fresh food from our monthly shopping trips could not have lasted more than a week and during the heavy rains when the Pungue River was running so high that it could not be crossed, we did not get into town for six to eight weeks at a stretch. And sometimes, particularly during the tourist season, we were simply inundated with visitors. But we made do as best we could. In the year before I acquired a freezer I had to rely on tinned or dried foods; and in fact I found a great deal of satisfaction in making something out of next to nothing and having to use my initiative to survive.

Eggs I used to buy in large numbers and if they did not last until the next town trip I could sometimes buy a few locally. Chickens too could be bought from the tribal people. We used powdered milk, a lot of cheese, and I used to make dishes using beans or rice and the locally grown millet, called *mapira*. I used whole grain *mapira* for a breakfast cereal, and in making bread, as wholewheat flour was unobtainable in Moçambique. The dried salted codfish, *bacalhau* so beloved of the Portuguese, was an excellent food to have on hand as it could be stored indefinitely (the whole house would smell like a fish market from one little piece of stored *bacalhau!*) Ken and I took some time to get used to this strong smelling, strongly flavoured fish but eventually we developed an overwhelming passion for the stuff. We came to realize why one of the most common and popular conversations between Portuguese people, male or female, was the hundred and one ways of preparing it. With plenty of garlic and olive oil there is little that can beat a well-prepared dish of *bacalhau*.

Occasionally we would receive a portion of meat from a buffalo that had been shot for the African staff or from a wounded animal that had had to be killed. Eland, wildebeest and elephant meat came to us in this way on rare occasions. Twice we were given a piece of trunk from elephant which had had to be shot as they had formed the habit of raiding neighbouring millet fields and were a danger to the local populace. Trunk is a popular portion to connoisseurs of elephant meat. It takes ten hours of boiling to get it tender but once ready it cuts and tastes much like tongue. Served hot with a Madeira sauce it is really very good.

During our second year in Gorongosa the owners of a farm on the park's southern boundary must have felt sorry for us and they very kindly gave us a paraffin-burning deep freeze. This made life much easier as I could freeze meat, eggs, or vegetables while they were plentiful. We became so enthusiastic about having a permanent supply of meat that we decided to buy a calf from our friends on the Gorongosa Mountain cattle ranch and freeze it. Ken went to fetch it in the Land-Rover and brought it back, skinned and cleaned but otherwise whole, wrapped in plastic sheeting. The animal was not a calf: it was a good bit bigger. We referred to it as the 'flayed ox' after the Rembrandt painting of that name. As the 'ox' had to mature before being frozen, it was necessary to hang it for several days. We could not leave it outside as the hyaenas would have made short work of it. There was only one place it could go and that was on our sleeping porch. So the carcass hung from the rafters of our porch dripping its ghastly juices on to the floor and spreading a dank sweet smell of meat through the house. I dreaded the thought of hyaenas discovering the scent and attempting to break in. Somehow the prospect of a pack of hyaenas howling and screaming round our bedroom seemed to me the most degrading and humiliating thing in the world!

However, the hyaenas did not scent it and after two days of the Gorongosa heat (although it was autumn at that time, it was still hot) the 'flayed ox' began to turn green. We quickly took it down; Ken cut it up and I washed and packed the pieces for freezing. Bacteria from the meat caused small sores on our hands to fester for weeks afterwards. The meat was duly frozen and although edible proved to be extremely tough! It had obviously not hung long enough.

Vegetables and fruit were readily available in the winter months at Chitengo. Perreira, one of the rangers, had an excellent vegetable garden which supplied greens for all of us for about four months of the year. During the summer pawpaws, mangoes and bananas were plentiful. The terrific summer heat used to scorch the vegetables though, and then neither Perreira's well organized *machamba* nor our scratchy little garden produced anything. I remember once picking the leaves off some poor weak carrots to make soup for Allan as he hadn't had anything fresh and green for weeks. The restaurant of the rest camp used to be able to help us with food during a crisis but mostly in summer they were in the same situation themselves, struggling to find something with which to make a meal.

Once a month Ken, I and the children went to Beira for provisions, gas for cooking, and paraffin for the fridge. During the summer when the roads might be under water and bridges swept away, the hundred

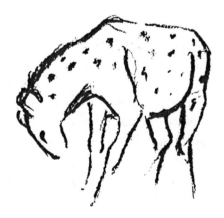

and twenty kilometre drive to Beira would take most of a day. In the dry season the Pungue River could be crossed by means of a floating plank and drum bridge, but as the river began to rise during the early summer rains the bridge had to be released and a pontoon was put to work ferrying traffic from one bank to another. Every vehicle traveling to and from the park or Vila Paiva to the north-west of us had to be poled over the swollen river. Ten bare-torsoed local men, lethargic and bilharzia-ridden, but wise in the ways of the Pungue and her currents, would use long, stout bamboo poles to push the pont upstream into the lee of an island and then let her float down with the current, guiding her until she beached at exactly the right spot on the opposite bank.

With a number of vehicles ahead it could take up to four or five hours to cross the river. And if you arrived too late at night, you just had to camp on the side of the Pungue until the pont-pushers came on duty again early the next morning. At the height of the summer floods the Pungue's waters were often too deep for the pole-driven pont to navigate, and a vehicle was usually kept on the far bank of the river for the park staff's use. We would then desert our vehicle on the Gorongosa bank and be rowed across in a small wooden boat, with the two children dangling precariously over the side and our bags and baggage resting in two centimetres of water at the bottom of the creaky old tub.

Our few days in Beira each month or six weeks were precious to us. Beira is a pleasant port built in a mangrove swamp which has been gradually filled in but has left a lingering heritage—a plentiful supply of mosquitoes. We soaked up the atmosphere of people, crowds, shops, and traffic after our near solitude in the park, and each trip was an adventure in itself. We often stayed for a few days in a block of beach flats so that we could enjoy the sea and the delightful freshness of its breezes.

Our favorite eating place was a small beach restaurant where we used to sit in the twilight, watching the moon rise over the old shipwreck that lay embedded in the beach sand near the lighthouse. Flocks of flamingo would honk over our heads as they flew across the bay. The steady breeze of the dark waters seemed to freshen up our systems and cool down our blood after weeks of the intense heat and humidity of the interior. As we walked back to our flat along the beach, phosphorescence would flame under our feet in the crisp wave-swept sand.

Once our shopping and any other business we had to see to was
completed Ken would load up the Land-Rover and we would head back
inland, by this time only too glad to get back to the park, despite the
heat, and away from the crowds again.

22

Babes in the Bush

Our son Allan was ten months old when we arrived in Gorongosa. It was difficult bringing up a baby in that tropical climate and doctorless region, but it was worth the battle and the worry. For Allan's first five years he grew up amongst animals and trees. A love of and interest in animals seemed to be innate in the child. When he was four months old we watched as he lay on his tummy on a rug in our Etosha garden and tried to put a pudgy forefinger on a column of tiny black ants that wove its way over a limestone boulder before him. In Gorongosa, as soon as he could walk, Allan began catching animals. Frogs were his favourite. In summer when the tadpoles in the rain pools had turned into baby frogs, those would be found all over the garden and often in the house too.

Allan's first words were 'Bite sore' and the Portuguese equivalent 'Morde'. His guardian Pedro and I anxiously tried to instill this fact into his head as his choice of captives became wider. However, he would cheerfully chant "Bite sore, bite sore' whilst determinedly going after the most dangerous of beasts. He found a baboon spider one day which had great hairy legs thicker than his fingers. He picked it up by one of these monstrous appendages and held it out to show me. The outraged spider reared up and bit him on the thumb. Allan dropped it fast but the bite was deep enough to draw blood. I never dreamt a spider could bite as hard as that. I sucked the wound to get the poison out and fortunately for the baby this seemed to do the trick as he had no swelling afterwards at all. (Months later one of the gardeners was bitten on the arm by a baboon spider and suffered a very painful and swollen arm for a week.) The discarded spider meanwhile was still furious, he did not attempt to flee at all but stood bristling and rearing up—he was so large that between his champing fangs I could see the pink of his mouth. I did not kill him but chased him as far away as possible.

Allan came to grips with a hunting beetle one day too—this is a fast-running ground-living beetle that shoots out a stream of acid if it is attacked. It shot Allan in the eye and I had a devil of a job to wash out the stinging poison using milk and warm water. He knew that *shongololos*—millipedes—were harmless but the attractive, bright red forest *shongololo* taught him differently by secreting a burning yellow substance all over his hands.

The boy met a baby waterbuck one morning on the plains. Waterbuck mothers leave their young concealed in a hollow or in a grassy patch whilst they go off to graze. We found this youngster lying as flat as it could on the ground, in a hollow, near the Urema Lake. Allan approached it carefully and we half expected the baby to take fright and run off but it lay motionless. Allan squatted beside it and stroked the warm head and soft velvety muzzle. The blond head of the boy bent close to the dark wild one as he talked gently to it. Then we left quietly so that the mother could return.

Allan has been charged by a hippo and—rather more seriously—by an elephant. He was walking with Ken along an arm of the Urema Lake when a lone hippo bull, feeling threatened as his protective water was rather low and he was somewhat exposed, charged out at them. Ken snatched up the boy and retreated but the hippo did not of course leave the water to follow up his charge.

The elephant charged down on us one day in the fever tree woodlands. We were all out of the Land-Rover and Allan was collecting the hard, dry pellets of impala dung and building castles with them. The tall bull elephant, taking umbrage for some reason at our presence, started screaming and rushing towards us from a long way away. I scooped up the toddler and bundled him into the car whilst Ken leapt in too and shouted and banged on the side of the vehicle. The noise brought the elephant up short. He shuffled around in the dust and shook his giant head so that his ears flapped. Lowering his head, he charged again but changed his mind suddenly and veered off in another direction.

I was against buying toys for my children, so Allan, and later his little sister Michelle, played with pots and pans, chunks of wood, pods and flowers, water, frogs, and whatever else they could lay their hands

on. Allan had a special sandy patch where he could make fires and he played with twigs and matches here to his heart's content. Of the more conventional toys he did have a teddy bear which his grandfather had given him on the day that he was born. The teddy did not receive very much attention until one night something happened to him that made him a very much more special kind of bear.

Teddy must have been left outside after we had all gone to bed and nobody missed him. About a week later a game guard brought me a mud-covered toy with an ear missing and asked if it belonged to my children. I said no, I did not think so. However, Allan recognized it as his bear. *Something*—probably a hyaena—had taken teddy off into the bush and tasted his ear. The game guard had found him some three kilometres from camp beside a waterhole.

During my pregnancy with Michelle, and her first months, I remember very little—I was too busy to keep a diary and too utterly miserable to write many letters. Pregnancy in a Rift Valley summer is like being a bloated tick in a tub of hot water. The pressure from within and without combines to make life seem totally unworthwhile.

Michelle was born in October of 1969. She was an unhappy baby as she suffered from a milk allergy for the first year of her life. We only discovered the allergy when she was five months old and then had to import a soya bean preparation as a milk substitute for her. During this difficult time Allan went through a stage of developing boils and blood poisoning regularly and tonsilitis every six weeks.

This worry of a sick child when one is living a day's journey from a doctor is worse than the illness in itself. The indecision of whether to make the dreadful journey to the doctor once again, or not, was harrowing. Usually, of course, we would end up going. The Beira doctors were an hour closer than the Zimbabwean doctors in Umtali (now Mutari) but from experience we had found the latter more efficient. Our only vehicle was a Portuguese official Land-Rover and this we were not allowed to take through the border into Zimbabwe. So from the border post we were in the habit of begging a lift into Umtali, some ten kilometres away. One day our lift was in the back of a poultry farmer's van—amongst the feathers and the droppings. Young Allan added his dropping too which contributed somewhat to the thickness of the atmosphere!

Late one Saturday afternoon when Allan was three years old, he fell with a stick in his hand and the sharp point stabbed him in the right eye. Ken was away on a trip to the Caborabassa region and I was alone with the two children. I gave Allan an aspirin and washed and covered the bleeding eye with a clean pad, but without a doctor there was nothing else that could be done. One of the rangers very kindly drove me to the Zimbabwean border and we arrived there at eleven that night, just before the post closed. Once again the official vehicle could not cross the border. I phoned our doctor from the post and arranged to meet him at the hospital. Then with a child on each arm and a bag of luggage at my feet I begged a lift from an elderly Umtali couple who had come across the border for a meal at one of the Portuguese restaurants and were returning home. Six hours after the accident Allan's eye was seen to by competent and kindly Dr. Kay. As the cut was very fortunately in the corner and had missed the pupil, his eyesight was not impaired and the wound quickly healed.

On several occasions I went alone to Zimbabwe with one or both of the children. Then I would travel in the diesel rail-car that ran daily between Beira and Umtali. A train-like car with driving controls both fore and aft so the driver could step down at the terminus and take over at the opposite end for the return trip, it could carry some fifty to sixty passengers but was seldom full. A Portuguese grandmother in inevitable black clothes, with her lunch in a paper bag, a young mother like myself with two or three unmanageable children, a few black women with bare feet and brightly coloured cotton wraps, would make up the usual quota of passengers. We would stop at most of the small stations along the way. They were often decorated with the blue and white tiles that the Portuguese love so dearly, and the platforms would be thick with dusty peasants and half-asleep railway officials.

In Umtali I would stay in a caravan in the garden of friends of ours, the Plowes. These people had a tame genet cat at one time and the daughter kept a pair of delightful African dormice in a cage in her bedroom. After I had seen the doctor or whatever else it was that I had to do, the Plowes would see me on the rail-car again and I would be heading once more into the primitive depths of Moçambique from the modern, neat and pretty little Zimbabwean town. But I would be pleased to be going back. Moçambique may not have been very progressive, the services not all that efficient (it often amazed me that systems such as the telephone and postal system ever worked at all!), but its undevelopedness appealed to us and we did not care if the roads were full of potholes and cattle, if the telephone lines were sometimes down, or if things were difficult to get. We liked it that way and it was home.

23

The Savannas

The wooded savannas that surround and encroach upon the floodplains of Gorongosa stretch up on the Rift Valley sides. They are made up of a mosaic of different tree species. Fever trees and winterthorn are dominant right next to the floodplains. Woodlands of the vast lemon-barked fever trees dwarf elephant herds beneath them, house troops of baboon and crested crane at night and spread an intoxicating and luxuriant perfume from yellow blossoms in the spring. The fever tree woodlands are among the most memorable parts of Gorongosa: the pale trunks and branches give them an ethereal quality, especially in the mist of morning or the blueness of twilight. The sight of the rising full moon behind their branches is one of exquisite delicacy and heartrending beauty.

Stands of lala and borassus palms take over where the fever trees and winterthorn leave off, and they in turn give way to other species of savanna trees. Tall and slender when mature and undisturbed, many of the palms are kept in shrub form by elephant that tear out the growing hearts, chew them up and spit out balls of the masticated tougher fibres. I had always intended to taste this 'heart of palm' and perhaps use it during the rains when we were short of fresh food, but Ken was not keen to let me aid the elephant in dwarfing the palms! The tough-skinned nuts borne by the palms are favourite food of elephant too—they roll the bigger ones underfoot in order to crack them.

Lone buffalo lurk amongst the palm scrub and constitute one of the greatest dangers to anyone on foot. They are usually old and bad-tempered, their hides dull, balding and shaggy with crusts of dried mud from wallowing—one of the last pleasures left to these old patriarchs. The cool mud soothes their itching hides and protects them from the incessant onslaught of biting fly. I am very fond of these old bulls. Their faces under the heavy eroded boss of the horns are craggy and graying: full of that brand of character that comes from a tough and virile life. Over a raised muzzle with distended and torn nostrils, such an old bull looks out with suspicion and curiosity, his ragged drooping ears fanning away the ever present flies. Ox-peckers creep unheeded over his shoulders and head, tearing off ticks and occasionally lumps of flesh too. Sweeping his tufted tail over his back produces puffs of dust as if from a dirty mat being beaten as he snorts and turns away from us—as if to say, 'So much for humanity!'

Buffalo have always seemed to me to be one of the symbols of the African wilderness, along with spiraling vultures and the call of the hyaena at night. There are a few more satisfying or primitive sights than that of a large herd of buffalo with the sun gilding the dust raised by their hooves and throwing intense shadows from their massive powerful bodies and the repeated curls of hundreds of horns. Herds of buffalo, sometimes up to two thousand, roam the Gorongosa floodplains whilst they are exposed. During the flooding the herds move into the tall grasslands under the savanna trees which, even when dry, provide fodder. These heavy animals trample down the grass in many areas and this provides a protective mulch for new young shoots to come through. If there is too heavy a concentration of buffalo or other large ungulates the grass may be destroyed completely and the soil, grass roots and seeds left unprotected, to be washed away by rain or blown by wind. The migrating buffalo herds are sometimes followed by prides of lion which become nomadic to make use of this moving source of food, tracking down the young, sick and weak. Lion usually have fixed home ranges but the nomadic lion move on whenever the buffalo move.

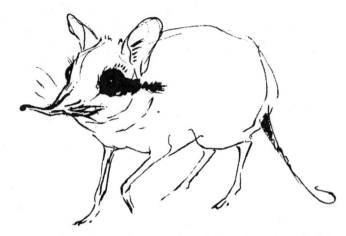

Lichtenstein's hartebeest (a tan-colored hartebeest) and sable antelope also occupy the grasslands of the savannas. Although they use the same habitat they are not usually found side by side. During the dry season most of the sable are found on the Rift floor whilst the hartebeest are in the hills. In the wet season the sable move up to the hills and the hartebeest are found in the valley.

Dotting the savannas are literally thousands of small seasonal pans which during the rainy season are filled with water and may house a hippo or even a crocodile. Used continuously by large numbers of game, the pans are often enlarged by their wallowing and trampling.

In summer as we drove through the savannas I was always astounded at the lush exuberance of the vegetation and how rapidly the grass had grown, especially around these little pans. The humid air would be full of the smell of growing things and rotting vegetation, and the grass would be brilliantly, almost luminously, green. At this time of the year white foam nests of the grey tree frog clustered like snowy fruit from branches overhanging the pans, keeping eggs safe from predators in the water. When the eggs hatch the tadpoles wiggle their way out of the slimy, bubbly mass and slip down into the pan. Grey tree frogs in our trees at Chitengo would tell us when rain was due, their crackling, croaking voices piping up suddenly and comically on a still evening.

Most years, by the time the height of the dry season is reached, the pans are again completely dry, frogs have gone into hibernation in deep cracks and seasonal fish and crustaceans are weathering the drought in a tough resistant egg stage in the dry mud. The hippo and crocodile have migrated back to the big lake, and surrounded by dry, brown vegetation our favourite living jewels are almost unrecognizable. If the water dries up slowly from these pans and is not drained out through deeply ploughed hippo paths or erosion channels, they have a green short-grass cover for most of the dry months and provide excellent and vital grazing for many of the ungulates. Zebra, wildebeest, waterbuck and elephant, even baboon, feed on these green islands for as long as they are available. Impala, bushbuck and others eat the weeds and herbs that shoot up in or around these pans. Rapid drainage from the pans leads to their premature drying out and the clayey soil becomes hardbaked and unproductive, depriving the ungulates of an important pasture resource and thus lowering the overall carrying capacity of the savannas.

Scattered around in the savannas too are clumps of thicket, growing mostly on the huge hill-like termite mounds. These are savanna trees and they form ideal habitats for such shade and shelter loving animals as the elephant shrew, the bush-squirrel, Heuglin's robin and red duiker. The elephant shrew that occurs in Gorongosa is big, about the size of a young kitten. It is a delightful animal, rust-red and grey in colour with the long rubbery, twitchy proboscis which gives it its name and with which it sniffs out insects amongst the bark and leaves, and elongated delicate limbs that step over the leaf mould with gazelle-like movements. We saw a pair of elephant shrew in the Beira zoo and I had a chance to examine and draw them; in the bush they are seldom seen except for brief glimpses as they dash along their well-worn paths in the thickets or across the roads.

In the savannas, in areas of deep well-drained sands, a dry type of forest occurs with true forest species of trees and understorey, but with few epiphytes such as lichens, orchids and ferns in the crowns. These patches of sand forest are well used by buffalo and elephant who love the deep shade during the heat of the day. Nyala, bushbuck, the brightly polished red duiker and the tiny suni antelope live here; families of bushpig bulldoze their way through the thicker parts in order to look for fallen fruit or edible roots. These forests are among the few places in Gorongosa where the tsetse fly occurs, here and in the woodlands of the Rift Valley sides. Fortunately they do not carry sleeping sickness as the disease has for some inexplicable reason never spread south of the Zambesi River.

To walk along game trails through the quiet of the sand forest was for us always infinitely rewarding. The canopy leaves whisper and sigh softly, talking to themselves and anyone else who has the inclination to stop and listen. During winter the deciduous trees of the forest shake veils of yellow leaves down into the undergrowth from which comes the bright song of the bearded robin. Overhead flocks of trumpeter hornbills shatter the peace with their wailing infant-like cries.

A Portuguese-Indian student from Portugal who was doing a University vacation project at Gorongosa was once terrified out of his wits by these hornbills. We were walking in the prehistoric atmosphere of the forest with the late afternoon sun deepening the shadows when a flock of trumpeters started up their human-like wailing. In terror Rosario raced back to the Land-Rover, leaving us completely bemused. Shaking, he explained that he was positive the crying must come from witches or demons. He was not reassured, even by three-year-old Allan's complete lack of fear or concern.

Whereas lion, along with hyaena, jackal and cheetah, are predators of the floodplains and savannas, the leopard is the hunter of the forests and woodland. Gorongosa has a high population of leopard and the lovely silent cats are often to be seen stretched in dappled sunshine along the branch of a tree or padding silently along a track. Crowned eagle is another predator of the forests, living off monkeys, squirrels and suni antelope.

The tropical Gorongosa savannas are not unique nor overly productive in animal life but it is their combination with the huge areas of floodplain which makes this system so rich and distinctive. However with the spiral of years and the natural or man-activated diminishing of the flooding region the plains are shrinking. The day they are lost and the savannas take over completely is the day Gorongosa will lose its diversity of animal life—if man has not in his crude and thoughtless way ensured its destruction already.

24

A Sea of Trees

An exciting and attractive part of the savanna system in the Gorongosa area is the *Brachystegia* woodlands. The genus *Brachystegia* includes several species of trees that often grow together over vast areas, dominating tracts of woodland which the local people call *miombo*. Along the Rift Valley sides near Gorongosa the *miombo* grew in a sea of trees unbroken except where shift cultivators had cut and burnt a clearing to plant their crops.

The *miombo* is especially remarkable for the bright colour of its new leaves in spring. Whole trees flame with pink, orange, red or russet once the new leaves have unfurled. Among the most beautiful sights of Zimbabwe are the hillsides ablaze with these burning colours in August or September. In moister Moçambique the arrival of the new *miombo* leaves is not as well synchronized and individual trees are colourfully decked rather than whole communities of them.

The valley mists which occur in winter and high humidity of summer enable a great number of epiphytic orchids and ferns to grow on the trunks and branches of the Gorongosa *miombo*. From trees felled along a roadside, we collected twelve different species of orchid and tied them to one of the mango trees outside our house at Chitengo. These plants produced a startling variety of flowers—showy spotted flowers, pearl white bridal-like flowers with elongated spurs, minute greenish yellowy flowers, and the most fascinating of all, spikes of little purple and brown blossoms with furry tongues that quivered in the wind and looked for all the world like minute, grotesque insects rather than flowers! Lemon yellow and purple aromatic ginger-plant flowers could also be found in the *miombo* during spring, growing out of the moist leaf mould in protected sites.

Miombo woodlands are seldom rich in game, the grasses being coarse, acid, and lacking in nutrition. Sable antelope and hartebeest do use them, however, and occasionally elephant and buffalo. Like so much of Moçambique, the Gorongosa *miombo* is subjected to fires every dry season. Tall flames from the dry grass below rake the lovely trees, sometimes leaving them as blackened skeletons growing with embers for many days, or as grey wraiths of ash laid out in the old shape of the trunk and branches on the sooty ground.

In January one year we took friends into the *miombo* on the eastern side of the Rift Valley, a section which is known as the Cheringoma plateau. We went for the day and I packed lunch for us all. Unfortunately I had underestimated how much liquid we would need in the mid-summer weather. I had two flasks of lemon tea and a bottle of water for the children.

We set off early while the day was still fresh—as fresh as the stagnant summer air could be. The Urema River, which at other times of the year can be forded, was running high and we crossed on the pontoon newly established there. The pont looked very unsafe to me, being little more than two planks nailed on to six empty petrol drums, and it was only just longer than the Land-Rover it carried. However despite my trepidations we were pulled across quite safely, bumping as we went floating past islands of blue flowering water hyacinth and white water lilies. Once before whilst fording this river our Rover scooped up piles of hyacinths on the front bumper and tangled among them was a very large and surprised barbel, his fishy whiskers bristling with indignation!

The track up on to the Cheringoma ran through patches of dense sand forest. We stopped in the shade of one of these to investigate some beetles Ken had spotted. Tsetse fly found us but they were not numerous. Allan discovered a nest of hairy caterpillars which he gathered in his small grimy and sweaty palm and allowed to walk over his bare chest and shoulders. To our surprise caterpillars have never yet stung him despite his continual disrespect for their stinging hairs and his predilection for collecting and petting them.

Further on through the *miombo* woodlands we stopped in a wide grassy dell, or drainage basin, where the water draining off the surrounding sandy soils forms a waterlogged glade on which tall rank grass and sedges grow. We set off after our own particular interests without worrying much about danger, as game is scarce in the acid pastures of these hill woodlands. After a while I discovered a pure gold lily frog, no bigger than a cent piece, nestled in the heart of a lime-green ginger plant. I gave a shout of delight at this exquisite find; the others gathered around to look at it and at that moment Ken stiffened and said 'Buffalo'.

About twenty metres from us a young buffalo stumbled out of the woodland, obviously very sick and in search of water. We stood still but he was too ill to be aware of us. Vasco, the game guard, was near the Land-Rover and he snatched up his rifle; but it was not necessary. The buffalo sank down into the long grass at the edge of the shallow water and we lost sight of him. How fortunate he was not there half an hour earlier! One of us, even one of the children, could very easily have stumbled upon him, and his horns were large enough to have proved very dangerous indeed. We walked quietly back to the Rover, filled with new respect for this bright world which can be so merciless to the unwary or the weak.

The waterfall where Ken took us to have lunch had honey-coloured water sifting through rock pools and sliding down a green algae-covered slope into a lake below. Tiny fish darted in and out of the rocky shallows, and leaves from the trees above floated down and made boats for the children to play with. It was two in the afternoon and desperately, crushingly hot. With lunch we drank every drop of the tea—and were still thirsty. The children had long since finished their bottle of water. Michelle was in fact slightly feverish and I soaked a hanky in the middle of the fast moving stream and laid it on her forehead. We did not want the children to drink water from the stream as bilharzia is very common in this area. We had no matches to make a fire.

The two-hour drive back was a nightmare. The exhausted children tried hard not to complain too much about their burning thirsts, for which I could do absolutely nothing. I cursed my lack of foresight and prayed we would not have a breakdown to delay us still further. At last we arrived back at the Urema pont and I asked the game guard if he could give us some water. He brought some immediately, cool and crystal, in a black clay pot, and we all drank deeply from it. Then I realized how silly we were. We had not drunk from the stream in case of bilharzia and yet here we were in our desperation drinking water without having any idea where it had come from! Thankfully we suffered no ill effects.

25

Drama on the Mountain Slopes

Travelling up from the Rift floor along the winding gravel roads to Vila Paiva, a village that lies just outside the western boundary of the park, you pass for most of the way through tall, dense *miombo* with patches of indigenous bamboo and hanging bunches of stag-horn fern and then suddenly out on to grassy plateaux at the base of the Mountain. Shifting cultivators have cleared and burnt patches of the woodlands for their gardens all the way along the road, and partly up the slopes of the Mountain one still passes plots of millet and maize. As the slope becomes steeper the gardens and habitations are left behind except for an occasional clearing biting into the forests in the gorges. The air becomes cooler as you rise above the plains, and in summer mist and rain shroud the peaks above. The coolness is a balm after the stagnant humidity below; the clear tinkling streams of amber water are irresistible—and at this height bilharzia free, so that you may splash in them to your heart's content.

On the second plateau, halfway up the Mountain, is a cattle ranch that has been carved out of the wild slopes by a tough pioneer rancher, John Wright. In our first years in Gorongosa John and Cynthia Wright were the only other English-speaking people in the region and we became very friendly with them. Later Geoff and Ailleen Harrison from the highlands of Kenya took over the ranch from the Wrights and they too became close friends of ours. Their hospitality, enriched with the fresh milk, cream, meat and vegetables that they produced on the ranch and which were such luxuries to us, was boundless.

The cattle ranch has had a sad history since John Wright struggled to open it up, building his own roads and house and importing woolly-coated Brangus cattle which were well suited to the cool moist climate of the Mountain. These cattle had to be injected once a week, a formidable task, against nagana (a form of sleeping sickness that attacks animals) as tsetse were present in small numbers on the forested slopes. Hyaena would sometimes kill calves and one night a misguided hunter shot a full-grown cow, mistaking her by torchlight for a kudu! The Wrights built a dwelling consisting of five separate rondavels—a delightful rustic place with cement and mud floors and thatched roofs. For many years they worked at improving the ranch, transporting cattle for market all the way down the Mountain across the Pungue by pontoon and then on over the one hundred kilometres of bumpy road to Beira. They enjoyed the life for all its difficulties, and one of the greatest of these was labour. The local workers gave continuous trouble.

The Che-Gorongosa people are cultivators and not cattle people. They did not relish the work of the cattle ranch and absenteeism and irresponsibility was rife. However one of their staff, the man who worked in the kitchen, was hardworking and reliable. For years Jim worked for Cynthia in the house, tending to the cooking, cleaning, lighting the paraffin lamps at night and ensuring that the water supply from a small stream above the house flowed efficiently. Then Jim took ill, the local

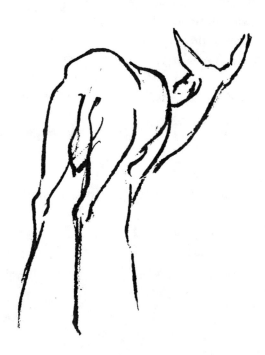

hospital diagnosed a venereal disease, and he was given sick leave so that he could receive treatment.

Early one morning, just after dawn, when the air of the Mountain was cool and moist and the sun was just tipping the rain forested slopes above the ranch, John was paying his staff their month's wages. Jim arrived unexpectedly. His behaviour was unexpected too, and alarming. Ranting and threatening, he approached John brandishing a large heavy stick. The elderly rancher asked the other labourers to get rid of him but they could not do so and when Jim refused to calm down or take himself off John went indoors to fetch a .22 pistol in case of more trouble. No amount of talking would get rid of the cook, whose mind seemed to be completely deranged; so John produced the gun and fired a shot at Jim's feet. This got him moving and he trotted off down the road. John fired another bullet into the ground to make sure he would not come back.

The second bullet unfortunately hit a stone, and unknown to the onlookers, ricocheted and hit the labourer in the back. Giving absolutely no sign that he had been struck the wounded man walked to a neighbouring farm and received a lift to the hospital in Vila Paiva, some fourteen kilometres away. At the hospital he did not receive treatment until the next day and later died of peritonitis.

John Wright was immediately taken into custody and jailed, as the Portuguese law maintained a person was guilty until proved innocent. He was taken to the Vila Pery jail, some hundred kilometres away. We visited him there and were horrified to find that the jail consisted of a rough tin shed in which nineteen black prisoners, ranging from murderers to petty thieves, were confined. Fortunately the warden took pity on the elderly man and allowed him to sleep on a stretcher in his office. For more than four months John was penned up in this filthy primitive prison awaiting the verdict. At last the report from the ballistics expert confirmed that the bullet had in fact ricocheted, and the poor man was released on bail.

John and Cynthia Wright could not bring themselves to return to the Mountain or to Moçambique. They settled once again in (what was then) Rhodesia, where John was killed some six years later by a landmine whilst on police reserve duty.

The Harrisons and their two teenage children lived on the ranch for several years, building themselves a new house and introducing the humped, milk-skinned Brahman cattle to the herds.

In 1973 when the guerrilla war being waged between Frelimo and the Portuguese army reached Gorongosa the Harrisons had Portuguese troops stationed at the ranch and they had to barricade their house every night. Twice the family's Land-Rover was ambushed by guerrillas and a young man who was helping them run the ranch was very nearly killed by machine gun bullets. At last they were forced to move from the Mountain, taking their cattle with them, to a ranch on the plains nearer to Beira. Their lovingly built house was ransacked and burnt soon after their departure.

But these tragic happenings were still in the future when we got to know Gorongosa Mountain and first climbed her forested slopes. She was like a mother figure. Her long blue-hued shape was always conspicuous above the plains and low hills of the Rift Valley; the relative dryness of the Valley's climate was offset by the everflowing life-giving streams that poured from her and perennially filled the channels and lakes of the plains.

26

Rain Forest and Summit Moorland

For a whole year whilst we were in Gorongosa Ken used to climb Gorongosa Mountain once a month to record the phenology (the times of flowering, fruiting, leaf-fall of each species) of the summit vegetation. On a few occasions I was able to join him, having left the children at the ranchhouse.

It was a two-hour climb, or rather a stiff walk, along a steep, damp but well-defined path up the southern side of the mountain to the highest peak, Gogogo. After entering the forests the path crept up between towering silent trees which were encrusted and dripping with brilliantly emerald ferns, grey 'old man's beard' lichen and tier upon tier of orchids, small aloes and other plants germinated in, and fed by, the thick mats of vegetable matter caught in crevices and forks of the branches. Soft-leaved, pink-and-mauve-flowered balsam and labiate plants covered the floor with here and there a delicate bamboo-like forest grass.

Trudging slowly up and up over the thick leaf mould we examined the plants beside the path for snails—land mollusks being one of the animals that Ken collects and uses as 'indicators'. Frogs and bloodsucking flies are the other animals of which he makes collections as the distribution of particular species fits rather closely to particular environmental conditions. On one occasion we found two small forest snails in the balsams—one of them a carnivore with spiny protuberances on its shell. This was the first I had ever heard of snails being carnivorous, let alone cannibalistic as this one is—it sucks the juice out of captured fellow snails—and it made me look at these seemingly inoffensive soft-bodied animals with new eyes.

Another specimen, which was a quarter the size of my small finger nail, had a little wriggly upright tail on the end of its body which it could wag exactly like a puppy. It made me glow with an excitement as great as if we had discovered a form of life never before seen by man. It was so new and strange—so totally unexpected—to find a pink tail-wagging mollusc tucked away in these silent dusky recesses of our world. The snail might be perfectly still, mute and rather obtuse as all snails are, but that delightful tail on the end of the translucent body thrashed expressively from side to side!

Standing there in the vast rain forest filled with countless forms of life, all completely independent of the presence of man and his works, I could not help feeling how insignificant we really are in the basic scheme of things and yet how much we miss by not being more a part of it. To me it seemed that to be able to know the function of that wriggly little tail was important—to all of us. To look at the snail and his form not from a coldly objective and scientific point of view, but rather as a connoisseur of life forms and natural adaptations.

There is so much interest and inspiration to be captured from the, as yet, unfathomed variety of animals and their habits. As one digs deeper into man's knowledge of the natural world it is astounding to see how little is known about even the more conspicuous animal and plant life. Insufficient knowledge and awareness of the existence, relationships, and behaviour of other life forms prevents us from sharing or participating in this great web and absorbing a meaning from it for our own lives—as well as a wealth of stimulation conducive to a creative level and a maturity that we have not yet reached. Western man has become so egotistical,

so preoccupied with himself, that his cultures are becoming inbred and stagnated, and he continues aimlessly to search his own soul for novelty, originality and meaning. An injection of vitality, inspiration, excitement and above all meaningfulness is needed from without, from that which is not man-made, from that which is greater than us.

As we climbed, the forest trees whispered softly under an occasional breeze and the branches shook violently when we disturbed a troop of feeding tan and black samango monkeys. Far off a green-crested turaco sounded, its hoarse throbbing call echoing in the forest. A stream sang, and then as we rose above it the humid silence closed around us again. Near the top of the mountain the path left the dank greenness of the forest and wound upward through a belt of mountain cedar and heath thicket and around huge boulders. Aloes with crimson spears sprawled over the rocks and in moist humus-filled hollows a minute dark purple ground orchid was flowering: a moss orchid, that grows amongst those communities of dwarf plants adapted to the moss and lichen mats of rocks.

At last the grassland of the plateau and saddles on the top of the mountain came into view and I stumbled up after Ken and threw myself down into the bronze bracken-scented grass. The air was rarified up here—1800 metres above the plain, clearer and thinner. On both sides of us rose rugged outcrops of fine pink and grey granite etched with dark humic stains and scattered with silver-green tattered palms of *Strelitzia*, the wild banana. Far between the outcrops the soft yellow grass stretched up on to the next peak. The impact of such startling wilderness, such positive, humanless naturalness, plus an exhilarating purity of air made me catch my breath and tears burnt my eyes.

The top of Gorongosa Mountain, after several visits, became for me the epitome of unsullied wildness. After our long climb through the dense, humid and dripping rain forests, the temperate glades of grass and bracken, the scented leaves of crisp yellow everlasting daisies underfoot and the piping of grass birds around us seemed incongruous— giving an impression of coming out into a Conan Doyle's *Lost World*.

The stinging morning sunshine does not last long on top of the mountain: a little before or after midday misty clouds caused by the rising of the warm sea breezes over the massif settle and drift amongst the grey rock peaks and the delicate banana fronds. Then the golden grasslands begin to look like misty Scottish moors with patches of weak sunshine and shrouded ghost-like clumps of trees and rocks.

No people at all live on the top of the Mountain; and Ken's recommendation that the whole of the massif be included in the boundaries of the park was accepted later in our stay in Gorongosa. There is not much large game on top of the Mountain and it is very seldom conspicuous: a few reedbuck, grey duiker, leopard and lynx. Rock hyrax do abound, and red rock hare. On rare occasions Ken has seen elephant in the forests on the eastern slope of the Mountain, but they do not appear to climb right up to the top.

It rather surprised me that the local tribal people did not climb the Mountain more frequently—although there was perhaps not much reason for them to do so. Traps were set within the rain forests for blue duiker and bushpig, but there was little else to be hunted and only an occasional hunter or medicine plant gatherer would climb the steep paths.

There are legends amongst the Che-Gorongosa tribe of a race of small people who used to live on the Mountain long ago. Quite possibly these 'dwarfs' were the bushmen who were displaced from the plains and forced on to the shelter of the Mountain in the far off times when the Bantu tribes moved south and occupied the area.

The Mountain is held somewhat in awe by the Che-Gorongosa people although it does not seem to play a conspicuous part in their worship or beliefs. They say that at times it growls and roars from deep down in its belly. Once in the woodlands near Vila Paiva we felt and heard the roar for ourselves. It was an earth tremor that lasted about half a minute and rumbled from the direction of the Mountain. The Mountain is not volcanic but the faulted sides of the Rift Valley are still unstable and some movement does occur along them from time to time.

On the occasions when I climbed the Mountain with Ken we ate our lunch—sandwiches and fruit—on the summit looking down over the humidity-hazed plains of Moçambique below. One afternoon we had the improbable fortune of rounding off the meal with excellent filtered coffee and cognac. As we sat eating a huge sweating hulk of a man had staggered up the steep path with a retinue of a dozen black porters—a sight straight out of the last century. He was a trig surveyor who was to spend a week on the Mountain. Judging by the prodigious amount of equipment and food that he had brought along with him he might have been going to spend three months there. Before our horrified eyes his people began to hack a niche out of a thicket for a camp and release half a dozen chickens to run around until required for a meal. Then this amazing example of Europe in Africa, totally unfazed by coming across two white foreigners who could speak Portuguese in this most unlikely place, beamed at us with an aura of garlic and *bonhomie* and sat down at a wooden table to a four-course meal, starting with soup and ending with the coffee and cognac which he invited us to share.

How amazing it is that people so often behave like tortoises, carrying their houses around with them—even if they are a little cumbersome. They have no wish to adapt to unfamiliar conditions and mould themselves to fit the new niche in which they find themselves; they cling to their own language, their own national foods and habits even if they have to struggle to do so.

The walk down the Mountain was of course quicker than the climb up but it still took about an hour and a half to make the descent.

One misty, drizzly day we had left the top late and before we were halfway down it was already quite dark. We had only one torch between us. However, the path was fairly well-defined and with Ken in front to shout out when there was a rock or tree trunk across the path I managed very well. I had taken off my canvas shoes as they were pinching my toes, and made the descent barefoot. Because of the soft leaf carpet of the forest floor there were few sharp edges that could pierce or bruise one's feet.

The forest was absolutely dark inside, I could see nothing apart from the light tan of the canvas pack on Ken's back. We were at last almost at the edge of forest and began to come across scores of fireflies flickering in the gloom. The insects did not appear to penetrate deep under the cover of the trees but kept to the ecotones between the forest and grassland. Their tiny greenish-white lights flitted silent and fairy-like around us, dipping and gliding against the intense black backdrop of the undergrowth.

27

The Field Research Station

The field research station at Chitengo was Ken's pride and joy when it was at last completed. The Veterinary Department, of which Fauna and Flora was a division, agreed as soon as we had arrived that a small building must be put up for research purposes. They quickly went about having the cement blocks made and the shell of the building erected. From then on things began to slow down. In order to get the materials for windows, doors, shelves, light fittings, basins, and tables Ken had to make numerous long and frustrating trips to Beira. Even the paint had to be brought from town. He did a lot of the painting himself; and we grabbed this opportunity to paint over the lilac-hued bedroom walls and green living-room in our little house as well.

Once the long simple laboratory with the study at one end was completed Ken commissioned me to do a mural on the outer walls. With earth-red and black I painted African designs on the white walls and a stylized nyala (a forest-loving antelope that is common in Moçambique), which we chose as the emblem for ecological research in this country. The woodland trees around the building threw patterns of dappled sunlight and shade on to the rough white walls. Squirrels scurried up and down these trees and came cautiously to drink from the natural rock bird-bath that Ken set up.

A pair of Heuglin's robin and morning warbler used the bath too. The robins lived in a thicket near the study, but the warblers came from nearer the house where they used to nest under the thatched roof and wake us every morning with their musical song and catchy signature tune—'te dee-dee diddle de dee'. Paradise flycatchers nested around the house and laboratory too. Small rust-red and blue birds, the males with long elegant navy-blue tails, they used to flash through the mango and cashew trees after each other, scolding in their imperative bell-like voices—animated hair ribbons, Ken called them!

Leopard used to roam the grounds after dark, we would hear their rasping call; buffalo, bushbuck and bushpig used to visit, and during the day a bad-mannered and noisy troops of vervet monkeys. Termites chewed their way into the timbers of the laboratory early on in its existence and after a month's holiday spent away from Chitengo we came back to find little earth tunnels along Ken's bookshelves and a few books badly eaten. Funnily enough the one most enjoyed by the termites was Eugene Marais' *The Soul of the White Ant.*

The laboratory building was as simple as possible but cool and pleasant to work in. By cool I mean relatively cool. In summer with the foliage thick and green around it and the steaming humidity emanating from the soil, the grass, and the bush even the laboratory was like a hot house, but this was a few degrees better than the sauna-like conditions around us.

Ken's staff consisted of two wiry black men, Signet and Vasco, of whom we became inordinately fond. Signet was the general help around the laboratory garden. At least, that was how he started out, but he soon became Ken's right-hand man on bush trips as well. He would help collect and press plant specimens, provide the local tribal names of plants and animals of which Ken always makes a list, and help with analysis studies.

Vasco was a much older man than Signet. Ken had heard of his reputation as a wily and knowledgeable tracker and when looking for

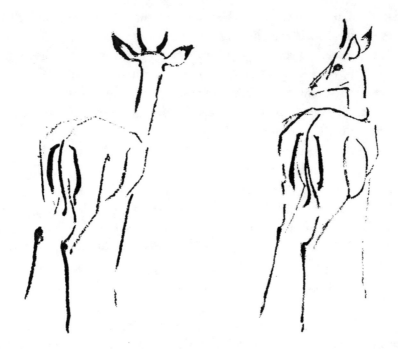

a game guard to accompany him on field trips he sought old Vasco out. Vasco was at that time living near Vila Paiva with his three wives and fourteen children, growing pumpkins, but was soon persuaded to come and work with Ken. I will never forget a visit we paid to Vasco's *kraal*. Most of his fourteen children are daughters, and when we arrived at the thatch and mud hut and the girls saw Michelle they swept down on her in delight. She was only two years old then and a blonde baby. The small fair head became swamped by the black woolly ones. Brilliant smiles flashed in the cheerful dark wave on which Michelle bobbed, a white seagull on a warm black sea. We went away with two large pumpkins as gifts.

Vasco was a musician. He had a thumb xylophone which was mounted on a calabash to give resonance to the notes and decorated with strings of cowrie shells that used to sizzle and jingle together as he played.

This bright-eyed little man was quiet and efficient, and a good hand with a rifle. He would keep watch, while Ken and Signet became absorbed in plant studies or digging soil pits, for the appearance of lion or elephant or any other danger. Animals are very curious and are often attracted by something strange, particularly if it is a rhythmic noise and movement like those of digging. Once attracted and at close quarters they tend to panic and can cause damage if anyone is in their way.

We had many visitors to the laboratory. The locals came to see the reptile collection that Ken had started (*uma cobra* has just as much horrid fascination for the Portuguese people as it does for black people) and often brought contributions of snakes with their heads smashed in. Once an

enormous green mamba was wheeled in in a wheelbarrow. This awe-inspiring specimen was over two metres in length and I can not remember who had been brave enough to kill it. Ken kept only the head and the rest was buried. A small mammal collection was also kept in the laboratory, and skins from rats, mice, shrews, and squirrels collected in Gorongosa by Steve Liversidge from Zimbabwe. An assemblage of local bird skins was housed here too, and a small herbarium of plant specimens.

Students on University vacations visited Gorongosa on several occasions and worked in the laboratory. Girls from many different countries working their way around the world or around Africa stayed for a while and typed for us. Typing and filing assistance was always very difficult to come by and for some reason we could never get a permanent typist who could speak English and who was willing to stay in *o mato* as the Portuguese called the bush.

28

The Dung Beetle Man and Others

One mild Sunday afternoon I was in the garden in front of the house with the children. The green pigeons were feeding in the giant sycamore fig tree above our heads and the purple-crested turaco were calling their timber-sawing call from amongst the huge crimson flowers of the sausage tree. I was rejoicing in the fact that there were no visitors to take Ken away that day, as so often during the tourist season our weekends together were ruined by people who felt they were entitled to be escorted around the park by the local scientist. If they were friends of friends or important guests Ken could hardly refuse.

On this day he was working in the back garden and we both anticipated having the afternoon to ourselves. However the outlook darkened as I saw two men strolling over to us from the tourist camp. They looked a lot like cranky Sunday bird-watchers and I groaned inwardly. The older man—tall, with khaki shorts, a bald head, and round glasses on a round and beaming face—spoke to me and of course asked if Mr. Tinley was at home.

'No,' I lied, 'I'm afraid Ken has gone out this afternoon.' The beaming face fell a little but brightened when Ken unexpectedly came around the corner. I felt horribly caught out, but like a mother hen trying to protect her family my blood was up: I did not feel remorseful but somewhat bitter and angry. The visitor either did not notice or was big enough to forgive me, as I know now he is. He started to explain to Ken who he was and we both, despite ourselves, fell under the spell of his fascinating story.

He was Dr. George Bornemissza of the Division of Entomology of the CSIRO in Australia: an entomologist specializing in the ecology of dung beetles. Some time ago he had managed to persuade the Australian government, after six years of repeated effort and evidence, that he had found an answer to the terrible fly scourge out there—in some places so bad that adults and children cannot go out of doors without a flyscreen around their faces.

The natural large fauna of Australia do not produce pats but hard pellets of dung, and the endemic dung beetles there have evolved to deal only with these and not with moist loose dung. With the introduction of livestock into Australia no corresponding 'waste disposer' existed. Australia was being covered with dung—the breeding place for flies; and what is more, in its dry climate, the fertile droppings were not incorporated into the soil but lay on top, dried out and blew away.

George had eventually persuaded his Division to send him to Africa to find and import dung beetles into Australia. Now, in his laboratory in Pretoria, South Africa, he breeds from collected specimens and the surface-sterilized eggs are sent to Canberra. This avoids the possibility of disease or parasites being introduced to Australia as well.

George had come with his assistant to Gorongosa to search for dung beetles, and Ken was able to show him the best places to find them. We were intrigued to hear that apart from sifting through the remains of elephant and buffalo dung and scooping out the specimens he also set baits made up of human or pig excreta. 'This explains,' said George, with the ever-ready twinkle in his eye, 'why I never eat garlic—the beetles can't stand garlic!'

One of the most efficient and fastest working beetles ever collected by this team was a chestnut-coloured specimen that was discovered disposing of pats of cattle manure at a rate of knots up on the southern slopes of the Gorongosa mountain ranch. George visited us twice at Gorongosa and we met him again in Pretoria, when we moved there years later. He had by this time married a British botanist and the two of them, although both in middle age, produced a brilliant and lovable son, Zolly, who has his father's round face and love for insects.

Near our house were several other staff houses. As is still unfortunately the case in game parks in Africa, the tourist camp and staff housing at Chitengo are not situated on the outskirts of the park but inside it—bringing problems of food, fuel, and building material transport, airstrip development, waste disposal and general living conditions into the wilderness and by doing so impairing some of its wild atmosphere and the very qualities that people wish to seek out.

The camp is, however, pleasantly laid out and the tourist facilities which are to one side of it are good. Apart from the director, three rangers, and Ken, who all worked for the Fauna and Flora department of the Moçambique government, there were four members of staff employed by the tourist company that ran the camp. Ken and I were the only English-speaking people but our growing knowledge of the Portuguese language enabled us to fit quite well into the little community without drawing us too far into the back-biting, back-scratching side of it which is inevitable in close-knit rural societies.

The staff would often meet on a Saturday or Sunday night on the long verandas of the restaurant. A guitar would be played and the emotional Latin voices would quaver with feeling to the lovely lyrics of their national *fado* folksongs. We would drink wine and hold discussions far into the night. The children too would be up late, playing around us on the cool lawns.

The game rangers were young Portuguese who were as much on the tracks of unattached tourist girls as on those of poachers. Martins was probably the most dedicated tracker of this sort, a rangy lethargic boy with good-looking features and soft flopping black hair. Manual João was another. He spent a lot of his spare time bullfighting in Lourenço Marques, and more time in the hospital recovering. José Tello, the game warden, had worked in the park from the days when he was the only white staff member. He loved Gorongosa and knew the country and the animals well. Madeira, the mechanic, was a favourite of ours. He was large and cheerful and the size of his *bariga* or belly was a constant source of interest and amusement to the children. Ingrained with motor grease and good humor, Madeira lived a life of his own at Chitengo, spending the nights amongst the black girls and the days, whilst working on the vehicles, arguing with their brothers and fathers about the prices.

During the six months of the year that the park was open to tourists we used to receive quite a lot of visors—sometimes too many! It was either a feast or famine as far as social or intellectual stimulation was concerned. For half the year we were completely devoid of new faces, new minds, new ideas—for the other half we were swamped.

One of our most famous visitors was introduced to us as 'an American journalist'. Ken was asked to show this man around the park as he was writing a series of articles on Moçambique and of course Gorongosa was to feature in them. Ken brought the elderly gentleman home to tea after their first run together and I was introduced to James Michener.

'You're not the Michener who wrote *Haiwaii?*' I asked, intrigued. It was indeed that well-known and brilliant novelist, many of whose books we both enjoyed.

We met astronauts, politicians, journalists and big game hunters from many countries in Gorongosa. Lloyd Mason Smith, a professor of desert ecology from California, stayed a while, and Kurt Wentzel from the National Geographic Society visited us several times. One of my favourite visitors was the amazingly romantic figure of Moçambique hunting history, Count Werner von Albensleben. A tall gaunt man with a rim of white beard edging a strong jaw along which the scars from old sabre wounds stand out, Werner is the visual epitome of a German Count and has a deep love of Africa and her bush after the half lifetime he has spent in Moçambique.

In our early days at Chitengo we had no furniture apart from four canvas camping chairs and two tin trunks on which we ate our meals. In this way we also seated and fed our guests, two of whom on separate occasions plunged through the rotting canvas of the chairs, their legs and arms waving helplessly in the air.

The most unpleasant guest we were ever to have in Gorongosa sat in one of those chairs one day at lunch with us. Like many men who live in the wilderness he wore no underpants under his shorts. Sitting opposite him I was horrified to see that a good section of his masculine appendages had fallen out of the leg of his shorts as he leant forward and was hanging down in much the way in which the male camel's palatal sack had emerged at Rundu. The only difference was that this was hairy! I was too embarrassed to tell him about it so had to put up with the apparition throughout the meal!

This man seemed to go out of his way to be unpleasant. He spoke in a loud nasal voice, hawked, coughed, and belched at every opportunity and worst of all, invited himself to stay. On the next occasion he invited himself *and* his wife to stay. They slept in the hut in the garden but she, every bit as eccentric as her husband, drifted into the house the next morning in a diaphanous pink négligé and engaged Ken in a literary discussion before breakfast.

One dry season we heard news that four white rhino were going to be brought up to Gorongosa from Zululand. The campaign started by Ian Player some years past to translocate rhino from the Zululand Parks, where they were plentiful, in fact becoming too numerous, to other parts of South Africa where they were rare or extinct had now included Gorongosa. We had hoped that Ken's brother John, who was then Game Warden at Mkuze Game Reserve, would accompany the rhino, and when the lorries were due to pass through Chitengo at 2 a.m. one June morning after a non-stop drive up from Zululand, we were ready with flasks of coffee. Ken followed them the extra forty kilometres to the holding pens which had been built out on the plains. We were disappointed that John had not been able to make the trip but the new rhino afforded us quite a bit of excitement anyway. They broke out of the insubstantial enclosure or *boma* the very next day and rushed off into the park. Two survived as far as we know but the other vanished without a trace.

A further consignment of rhino arrived a few months later. Martins, the dashing game ranger, went down to Zululand to accompany the convoy on the long trip through Moçambique and up to Gorongosa. The next we heard were dreadful rumours of a disastrous accident involving the rhino lorries; Martins' new wife Ines was beside herself with fear that he might have been hurt or killed. The next day we learned that Martins and the Natal Park's staff were unharmed, but the occupants of the fast-travelling sports car which had smashed into the foremost lorry had been killed outright. The rhino in the lorry had escaped from its travelling crate and created further pandemonium. Not only was it quite impossible to capture the rhino in the darkness, but its crate had been damaged and it had to be shot. The two remaining rhino eventually reached Gorongosa after having been poled across the Pungue River on the pontoon; the floating bridge could not take the weight of the lorries. One of the big creatures, a cow, did not survive but died shortly after arrival.

Believing her to have been pregnant and hoping to find why she died Ken and Costa, a ranger who had recently joined the park, decided to carry out a post mortem. A delightful Portuguese, Costa spoke a surprisingly excellent English with an Oxford accent which he had picked up while working in England for some years. We all drove down to the *bomas* together. By now the enclosures has been strengthened and the surviving rhino had not managed to break out. He was in the same enclosure as the dead rhino, and in order to be able to work on the body the men had to get him out and into the adjoining enclosure. No amount of banging or shouting would induce him to move. Eventually Ken and Costa jumped into the *boma* and tried to provoke him into charging them through the open gateway. Costa drummed his feet and shouted like a bullfighter, waving an imaginary cape. The rhino looked puzzled but hardly enraged. After much more play-acting on Costa's part and cheers from us the big bull was encouraged to charge and Costa fled, leaping up and over the *boma* fence in front of that dangerous horn. Once the rhino was through the gateway Ken slipped the poles across to close it off and it was safe to begin work on the dead cow.

Using an axe and cane knives to hack through the thick tough skin they found a foetus in the animal, a perfectly formed little rhino about three quarters of the way through its eighteen-month gestation period. It looked as if the mother had died simply from the stress of the long journey.

29

Animal Relationships

Baboon are undisturbed in Gorongosa and they roam the plains and the woodlands at will. At dusk, after a day out in the grasslands hunting for insects, roots and seeding grass heads, they saunter back to the shelter of tall trees for the night where they sleep huddled along the branches in the company of crowned crane and egrets. The females and the young go on ahead, the highly spirited children scurrying between their mothers, arguing and squealing. The old males stride behind, administering a cuff to the head of any youngster that comes too close. Ken once saw one of these old patriarch baboon rout a young, but fully-grown, leopard. The baboon charged silently with bared fangs and chased the cat into a dense thicket of young fever trees. A few minutes later the baboon emerged quite unscathed and unbloodied so presumably that leopard had not stopped to argue.

These primates are amongst the most fascinating of all animals to observe. Here in Gorongosa we had a superb opportunity to study their behaviour as they were so often in the open and they were completely unperturbed by the presence of human beings, especially if in a vehicle. They would carry on with their lives unhurried and unharried, and with the utmost dignity and self-confidence: feeding, mating, disciplining their children, and sorting out their social hierarchy in full view of anyone who cared to watch.

Whilst baboon feed they are very often joined by other animal species. These may be impala, elephant, warthog, wildebeest, bushbuck, or even birds. The feeding associations are formed mostly because baboon are messy feeders, disturbing leaves and fruit and sending them tumbling to the ground where they can be picked up by other animals. It is also possible that the baboon, alert and often strategically situated high up in trees, act as an early warning system when danger is near. It is a warming sight to see animals of different species, if not actively helping one another, then at least enjoying and using each other's company. We have seen a flurry of baboon in winterthorn tree send showers of the delectable dry twisted pods down on to an elephant's head and shoulders as he stood below calmly picking them up with his trunk and putting them into his mouth. Baboon, and other small animals such as mongoose and squirrel, in their turn use elephant too. They will pick undigested seeds from the heaps of dry straw-like droppings, or turn over the pats to find termites and beetles that are feeding on them.

Animals certainly understood each other's 'languages' to a certain extent, reacting to warning calls or excitement calls of species other than their own. The hadedah ibis and the goaway bird are notorious among hunters for their loud alarm calls which alert every animal within a wide radius. That animals do react with pure curiosity to others' alarm calls was illustrated to me one day by a delightful tableau in the Kalahari Gemsbok Park in South Africa. A leopard had attempted to catch a bat-eared fox by springing out at it from a patch of tall yellow grass. The fox, with quite incredible agility, had escaped and being more fleet of foot than the leopard, had soon out-distanced him. A group of other fox foraging nearby set up a plaintive and scolding 'Koww Kow' barking, and advancing on the now exposed and helpless leopard, they formed a wide circle around him and mobbed him as small birds will an eagle. The leopard was furious and embarrassed, his tail fluffed up and the white tip thrashed savagely; he darted at one of the foxes but was too slow. Then

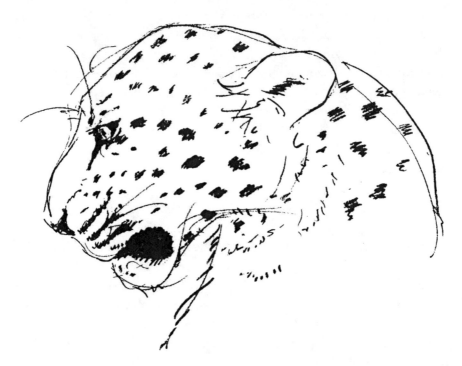

completely at a loss he stood, unable to advance or retreat, whilst the small animals kept up their mocking challenge.

From our vantage point nearby we could see a herd of springbok approaching the furor. Ears forward and with alert expressions they came to within a hundred metres and stood still to watch. A lone hartebeest lying some way off stood up to have a better look and then lay down again. Funniest of all to us was the fact that close to our vehicle a group of suricate mongoose had crept out of their holes and, perched on a termite mound, they sat straight up on their haunches with their inquisitive black eyes riveted on the scene.

The foxes dispersed after a while, the leopard padded off to the nearest tree and with one bound disappeared into its thick protecting foliage. The entertainment over, the audiences of springbok and mongoose went about their own business.

That animals of different species appear to benefit by or enjoy the company of others was the conclusion we had to come to from the hundreds of observations we recorded in Gorongosa. Ken has seen a group of waterbuck leave their resting place in the shade of a winterthorn tree and walk over a kilometer to join a herd of impala out on the plains.

The two herds walked towards the lake and then grazed together for some time. Lone wildebeest bulls will often join up with a herd of zebra or impala, seemingly for no other advantage than a social one. Impala and baboon enjoy warthogs' company, possibly because of the roots the latter dig out.

We sometimes saw some rather unusual associations such as red forest squirrel and red duiker feeding together and baboon with banded mongoose. Hugh Cott in his book *Looking at Animals* describes carmine bee-eaters, immensely colourful little birds, riding cheerfully on the backs of ground hornbill and hawking the insects disturbed by the bigger birds. The fork-tailed drongo does the same thing from the backs of rhino, elephant, or buffalo; and dragonflies will fly after an animal or vehicle in long grass for the minute prey that is flushed up in this way.

In summer when the sausage trees produce their plate-sized wine-red blooms baboon often frequent them, picking the flowers and drinking droplets of syrupy nectar from them. The flowers are then discarded by the wasteful primates and they drop heavily to the ground where bushbuck, bushpig or impala munch the juicy petals.

These examples illustrate a few of the fascinating inter-relationships that exist between animals. Some are seen and recorded, but how many go unnoticed; and how much can we at this stage deduce from the little that we have seen? There is obviously still an incredibly rich fund of knowledge all around us which as yet has hardly been peeped at by man—or is perhaps seen but still beyond his comprehension.

30

The Lions

Drive in the middle of the day a few kilometres along the edge of the floodplains of Gorongosa between the spiky fingers of the palm shrubs, and sooner or later you will come across a pride of lazy lion spread out in the shade like a molten mass of golden butter poured out upon the green sward. They seem to lead an easy life, these monstrous cats. Chins resting on giant forepaws, they turn their clear yellow eyes to gaze uninterestedly at the intruders. Perhaps a hint of curiosity crosses their amber depths—but no, it is too much trouble to get up to take a closer look. They flop back, swatting a spotted cub out of the way.

Ten kilometres from Chitengo was an old rest camp which the lion had taken over as their own. The Lions' Camp, as it became known, was a series of huts and a dining-room built many years ago as the first rest camp in Gorongosa. The site—on the edge of the floodplains—had been badly chosen and in the first summer floods rose halfway up the walls. Apart from the danger of flooding, the mosquitoes at that particular spot on a still summer's night must have been a living nightmare. The abandoned huts, whose whitewashed, regimented row stood out so starkly on the wide sweep of the plain, incongruously human in so primeval a landscape, became incorporated into the life of the plains by a large pride of lion who took it over as a home base.

We often visited the Lions' Camp in the late afternoons when the golden light and long shadows would stretch over the grass plains and rustling formations of ibis and egret flew over our heads on their way to roost in the riverine trees. We stopped some hundred metres away from the huts on the east bank of the deep channel that ran there and would sit outside or on top of the Land-Rover. The grass was short all around us and we had a clear view of any inquisitive lion who might attempt to approach; and at the same time we could look over the channel of water to the delicate blue shape of the mountain lying against the pink evening sky and to the herds of game stretched out on the plain before us. The children would play in the loose soil of the bank, throwing stones into the water and chasing insects.

Around the abandoned huts of the camp, the lazy lion lords rest in the open doorways and mothers and half-grown cubs climb the short spiral stair to the flat roof of the old dining-room. Here they presumably catch any slight breeze that may not reach the ground; they evade biting flies and have a good view of the grazing herds of wildebeest, waterbuck, and zebra. Any lone or crippled ungulate or lost foal can be spotted at once from this vantage point. A pinkly-shining hippo leaving the safety of the water for his nocturnal graze might also be seen and the pride activated to deal with him—a seemingly incredible feat of strength which is not uncommonly performed by the Gorongosa lions.

Young lion, as they angle their huge bodies around the bends of the stair—full-grown males are apparently too large to get up it—let loose with a forceful backward stream of urine at one particular spot as a token of proprietorship, leaving a wide grey stain on the fading white wall. Once on the roof the cats loll lethargically with paws or tails artistically draped over the edge. They gaze disdainfully down at the human viewers and scan the horizons at intervals to see if there is any sign of a meal that can be caught, or robbed from some other predator. Like most other animals lion will grab any opportunity that presents itself for obtaining an easy meal. They can be thieves and scavengers as well as hunters. In the Ngorongoro crater in East Africa where there is a large and active hyaena population the hyaena do the hunting and the lion has become a full time scavenger.

One morning Ken saw two young male lion sprawled out on a green patch of plain. A vulture circled unheeded above them and then spiralled down with outstretched legs to land a kilometre or so away. As they saw the bird land the lion immediately pricked up their ears, sprang up, and bounded away, like naughty puppies, to see what the vulture had found.

The lion often mate and rear their young around the camp, but during the dry season when the grazing herds leave the dried-out plains the carnivores follow and only return between intervals to the shady retreat of the huts. When in residence the lion commonly have a retinue of small hooded vulture lurking around their doors. These scavengers live to a certain extent off the dung of the lion. Some nutriment is still available in the excreta and, more important to the vulture, small pieces of bone. Vulture require the bone and the calcium it provides, particularly when they are fledglings and developing their own bones. Observations made of vulture in areas where there are few carnivores showed that chicks often have rickets or are malformed because of the lack of bone chips in their diet. In an attempt to supply these, impoverished parents bring home pieces of china, metal or plastic of the appropriate size! In areas such as Gorongosa, where carnivores are active, we always found great amusement in watching the scurvy-looking dark scavengers with their glittering eyes hopping around the grass and palm clumps, going about their dubious business and squabbling over a choice piece of dung.

The charm of lion themselves I have always found overrated. They are gorgeously beautiful, but they seem to rest upon this slight virtue and lack the of character of other carnivores such as the lithe and aloof cheetah, or the scampish wild dog. Their loose, flowing, relaxed lines— latently powerful as they are—I find less attractive than the tension of the clean-cut lines of antelope or the brusque silhouette of the buffalo. A lion stalking (we once saw a black-maned lion in Etosha repeatedly stalk a hare and repeatedly miss), is more stirring and impressive, but resting in the golden grass he is in fact just a shade too pretty. Lions' behaviour

backs up my impression of them as lazy, charming, but basically low characters.

On occasion during skirmishes they kill and even eat each other. The mothers abandon their cubs in the face of danger and even lack the foresight to carry food home to the weaned cubs: they will leave a kill and go back to fetch their young, leading the chubby cubs several kilometres through the roughest of terrain. By the time they return to it the prey has quite possibly been consumed by the adult males. It is no wonder that relatively few lion cubs ever reach maturity. This might be just as well as they have no enemies other than man and lack the susceptibility of other predators, such as wild dog, to diseases. So if lionesses were good mothers and male lion allowed cubs to eat before they themselves were full, Africa might by now have been overrun by these huge carnivores.

For all my jaded impressions of the big cats, a ginger-maned male in Etosha once gave me one of the greatest thrills of my life. This particular lion was renowned for his bad temper; and near a barren-edged waterhole one day he lost his temper with us for no other reason than that we happened to be driving quietly by. At a distance of fifty paces his tail started lashing violently from side to side, his yellow eyes sparked into a brilliance such as I have seldom seen, and in a bundle of deadly harnessed energy he charged. Our truck was always phenomenally sluggish in picking up speed, and never had it seemed slower than now with a violent lion coming at us like a whiplash and two completely unprotected game trackers on the back. We drew away and for a short while he kept on after the car; but then slowly he gave up. The trackers

were grey with fright: the memory of that angry lion will stay with all of us for life.

An interesting tableau that Ken and I witnessed late one afternoon in Gorongosa illustrated elephants' feelings toward lion. We noticed that a group of ten elephant cows and calves on the edge of the floodplain were uneasy. They were testing the air with their trunks and shaking their huge ears. Suddenly they seemed to come to a decision. Bunched together in a solid phalanx, with the calves on the inside, they charged down upon something lying in a patch of palm scrub. The something came out in a tawny streak. It was a large male lion, and with his tail between his legs like a mongrel that has been kicked, he rushed for the cover of a large thicket on a termite hill. The elephant milled around raising the dust and trumpeting. A lioness appeared from nowhere and in just as undignified a fashion joined the lion. They roared repeatedly, their voices mingling like cannons on a battlefield, but stayed where they were until the elephant moved off.

Lion do present some kind of danger to elephant calves, especially if the calves are injured or left unguarded by adults—which, however, seldom happens as they are so family conscious. This would seem to be the only explanation for such an unprovoked attack.

Late one night a pride of twelve lion crawled through the Chitengo camp fence very near to our porch. We heard the twanging of the wire and the irritated growl as one became hooked on a barb. As they padded past the porch we shone the torch through the wire netting at them. Twenty or thirty paces from us a couple of the young ones stood as the torchlight shone on them, looking into the beam, their eyes glowing eerily red. Then they followed the rest of the pride. I shivered to think how easy it would be for a lion to break into our porch if he wished. An effortless jump could take him over the one-metre wall and probably straight through the wire mosquito gauze. However I consoled myself with the knowledge that the large majority of lion would rather avoid man than seek him out as prey.

In fact I was to read years later in a chronicle written by Vasse, a hunter-naturalist, how renowned and feared the Gorongosa lion had been at one time, since many of them were man-eaters. Vasse was a Frenchman who visited Gorongosa in the last years of the nineteenth century and who ploughed into the large mammal population with an enthusiasm and a blood lust that is only compensated for by his written record of the country and times, and by the large numbers of scientific specimens, ranging from insects, plants and birds to the slaughtered mammals, that he sent back to a French museum. Vasse wrote that the people living around the Urema plains of Gorongosa used at that time to bow down to any lion they met or saw in the distance in order, they said, to appease it.

It was probably curiosity that brought lion into Chitengo's fenced camp that night and the visiting pride proceeded to enjoy itself. They lay down, cubs and all, on a small circle in the road and gave us quite the most unforgettable and deafening demonstration that I have ever experienced. Their roars from only fifty metres away rattled every window pane in the house: I was afraid they were going to shatter. For some reason the noise did not waken the children, for which I was thankful, as they would have been terrified. The roars woke practically everyone else in the camp however and soon to our distress we heard a Land-Rover starting up which proceeded to chase and harry the pride until they eventually, with complete loss of dignity, found their way out through the fence and back into the safety of the bush.

The Gorongosa Lions' Camp, which became so well known to visitors from all over the world, was bulldozed down recently by the new Moçambique government. Only the small dining-hall with its spiral stair was left standing and this is apparently no longer used as a shelter by the lions.

31

A Night on the Plains

Living in the bush does not bring as many adventures as people might imagine. We had relatively few exciting or dangerous experiences—although every drive out on to the plains or walk into the forests was thrilling and stimulating. Danger in the wilds can *usually* be averted by planning, watchfulness, and respect for the environment and Ken's amazing bush sense and bump of direction has always stood us in good stead.

One particular exciting incident however began, as these things often do, quite innocently. We went out late one July afternoon for a drive. I felt I needed an hour's break from Allan and Michelle, so I left them with a nursemaid I had recently hired. We set off for a short drive taking Signet and Vasco with us as Ken wanted to question them on the native names of some trees in the *miombo* woodland near the park entrance gate. We went through the tall woodlands and then around in a circular drive across the plains back toward home.

Suddenly the diesel Land-Rover, always kept in good working order by Ken and the mechanic at Chitengo, ran over a dry branch which by chance was flung up into the engine and broke the glass fuel feed-bulb. Deprived of fuel the engine cut out at once. The sun had almost set by this time. Its long pink rays washed over the plains picking out herds of wildebeest and zebra, and the mountain was retiring into a lilac haze. We were on *picada* five, one of my favourite tracks, which runs between towering baobabs and clumps of forest scattered over the tawny grasslands. There was nothing Ken could do to fix the car: the light was failing and the job was impossible without spares. We had no torch and no matches. We had no food, no water, and no jerseys to keep out the chilly winter air. We were therefore infinitely relieved to find Vasco had a

cigarette lighter in his pocket and after collecting branches from a nearby
dead tree he made a fire on the sandy road. For years after this the game
guards teased Ken as he had always scorned Vasco for smoking—now,
they said, where would we have been on that cold dark night on the
plains if Vasco had not been a smoker? In the gathering darkness we
huddled around the brisk fire and toasted our fronts whilst our backs
froze in the night air. I would have thoroughly enjoyed the adventure if
I had not been desperately worried about my children and the untried
nursemaid. I thought she would feed them and put them to bed but I
was worried that she might then leave them and go home thinking that
we would soon be back. We eliminated the possibility of walking back
to the camp as we were at least twenty kilometres away, over heavily-
bushed lion and elephant country. During the day it would have been
possible to walk but on a moonless night, even with a rifle, the risk of
meeting a lion or elephant unexpectedly was too high.

Curled up on a Land-Rover cushion in front of the fire I forced
myself to sleep. In the night a wildebeest came up to within a few paces

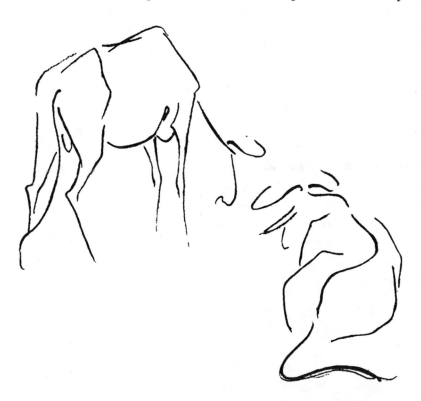

of us to investigate; his burp of surprise woke me. Baboons were crying and squealing in the sand forest a little way away. It was a terrifying sound and pathetically human. Ken told me that earlier he had heard a leopard's hoarse sawing call. It was the cat no doubt that had upset the baboons. Signet and Vasco, awake and watchful, pulled fresh branches on to the fire every so often when the coals were beginning to die down. The night passed eventually and the pearly mist that spreads over the plains on winter mornings diffused the weak rays of the sun and distilled in crystal droplets along palm spikes and grassheads. As soon as it was light we started to walk back to camp. The morning air was crisp and spicy; shapes around us—impala, palms, and fever trees—were veiled by the mist, now emerging, now shadowed, delicate and pastel. In places where the track was not sandy the hard clay of the dried floodplains was fissured and rutted, potholed by the giant tracks made during the rains by elephant and hippo. We walked about ten kilometres, silent, alone with our thoughts, the mist, and birdsong. At last we met a tourist car. We stopped and begged a lift back to camp for myself; it was a small car and could not have taken us all. Back at Chitengo with tears running down my face I burst into the house to find everything completely in order and the children hardly missing me at all. Both Ána the nursemaid and Pedro, Allan's companion and playmate, had slept at the house and the children could certainly not have wished for better care.

Ken and the guards walked back to camp. On the way they too met a tourist car. It was a huge low-slung American car and was filled to capacity with a family of South Africans. The driver seemed quite unsurprised at seeing a white man (Ken never wore a park uniform) and two blacks walking through the middle of a game reserve at six o'clock in the morning. Despite the fact that he was deep in Portuguese territory the Afrikaner blithely addressed Ken in Afrikaans asking where he could find lions. Without blinking an eyelid Ken answered him in Afrikaans, told him where the lions were and then the car and the walkers continued on their separate ways.

32

We Leave Gorongosa

During our four and a half years at Gorongosa, Ken had drawn up a plan aimed at securing the long-term survival of the park as a natural area, despite the rapidly changing conditions, and the people hungry for land and resources, all around it. The dam at Caborabassa to the north of us was almost completed. A dam on the Pungue near the southern boundary of the park was envisaged, and it would no doubt be only a matter of time before the expanding cotton and sugar companies began casting their eyes on the plains of Gorongosa as potentially irrigable lands for their cash crops. The local peasants shift-cultivating around the unfenced borders were forever encroaching into the, as yet, virgin woodlands and forests of the park. They built their *kraals* and fired new plots on land that they regarded as their own, having no clear idea of the real nature or practical purpose of a national park. Year by year there was a little more clearing of the precious forest-clad watershed of the mountain slopes from which came the very lifeblood of the system and on which the entire balance of the floodplains depended. Year by year thousands of wire snares were laid to trap the animals which the people from ages past had looked upon as being their rightful source of meat and hide, and no gazetted government statements or punishment would make them understand why this should no longer be.

Using his own experience and the information published by others in American and East African parks Ken put down on paper a complete plan for the future management and utilization of Gorongosa so that the surrounding people as well as the state could benefit from its prodigious natural resources and at the same time it might remain part of the cultural and aesthetic heritage about which conservationists all over the world prate so consistently but which means so little to the short-sighted and ever hungry peasant.

The plan was simple and required few material changes in the park setup but large-scale changes in attitude on the part of the controlling departments and the people living in the area. Gorongosa was to be divided into two: one section was to be a complete wilderness area in which there was only one access road, and was to be visited only by those wishing to experience wilderness or by those wishing to study aspects of it. The other section, the more southern one, and the one which in fact at that time contained the tourist roads, was to be for general tourist and educational viewing. Tourist camps were to be encouraged on the outskirts of the park among existing villages, and to be run by private enterprise. Cropping schemes were to be implemented by the park authorities and guided along scientific lines so as not to damage but to ensure the continuation of healthy and balanced populations of the more numerous ungulates such as buffalo, hippo, wildebeest and elephant. The local populations were to have access to meat from the cropping schemes and the whole region was to benefit from the various monetary incomes of the park.

The implementation of this plan would have meant that the Gorongosa ecosystem in all its natural diversity could have been a valuable part of the regional economy—and remained so forever, free from the pressures of land and resource grabbers and exploiters.

These recommendations, with those for enlarging the National Park to include the water catchments of the Mountain, and a strip across the Cheringoma Plateau to the sea, were approved by the authorities; but no definite action was taken or even seemed imminent. We therefore felt that being based in Gorongosa, a thousand kilometres away from the head office, was preventing Ken from having any influence on the decision-makers. So reluctantly he asked for a transfer to Lourenço Marques.

By July of that year, 1972, the guerilla war that had been raging in the north of Moçambique between Frelimo insurgents and the Portuguese army was getting alarmingly close to Gorongosa. We heard increasing accounts of landmines blowing up vehicles on the roads north of the park, of burnings and shootings that showed the steady spread of the movement southwards.

These developments and Michelle's ill health precipitated my own move with the children, and we traveled down south. Months later Ken joined us and visited Gorongosa again the following March for two months' field studies. During that time eighteen people were killed or kidnapped on the periphery of the park. Those two months were a strain for Ken.

With Vasco and Signet he would drive out at first light to the site where he wished to carry out the vegetation analysis which remained the uncompleted facet of his ecosystem study. Working steadily throughout the day with Vasco and his rifle ever vigilant for animal or human intrusion he would stop only when the sun had set and the light was too poor. Making a small fire which could not be detected from a distance, Signet would prepare the evening meal and the three of them would retire quietly and apprehensively into their sleeping bags. The next morning before the sun had risen they were away to the next site, Vasco having discreetly enquired of any local inhabitants about possible danger.

One morning as Ken was packing the vehicle to move on, three black men walked unannounced out of the bush towards them. They wore ragged camouflage and carried well-oiled machine guns. Ken's heart stood still. The Land-Rover had the DSV number plate of a government vehicle, so he could not pretend he was visiting *estrangeiro* scientist. A government official had that week been kidnapped and his camp and land moving equipment burnt, near the southern boundary of the park. The leader of the trio spoke first and asked who Ken was and what he was doing. Ken replied calmly in Portuguese, his mind working overtime on how to get out of this predicament if things became nasty. 'You can relax,' said the black man, 'we too are working for the Portuguese government.'

They were members of the 'Flechas'—a group of toughs and repatriates fighting Frelimo under the D.S.G. secret police department of the Lisbon government. Flooded with relief Ken shook their hands heartily and offered them coffee and breakfast. They told him that it would be better if he did not work alone in the bush any longer and from that time he withdrew to Chitengo, having to abandon a small section of the vegetation work that was still to be done.

Shortly afterwards he left, and about a week later an unpleasant incident occurred in the restaurant in Chitengo. One night the headwaiter, an elderly black man who was known as Tikki, beat the drum as he always did to announce that dinner was ready. The drumming seemed longer than usual and soon after it stopped the guests—including some Portuguese soldiers—started moving in through the wide doors of the restaurant. It was then that machine-gun fire rang out. Bullets whizzed through the open doors, breaking crockery and entering the ceiling and walls. People still out on the verandas fell flat or crouched behind tables. After the initial two or three bursts the shooting died down.

The Portuguese soldiers in the meantime grabbed their firearms and started searching for the attackers who were hiding in the shadows. But they escaped into the darkness and must have left the park by crossing the Pungue River.

We heard the Tikki was jailed for his part in relaying through his drumming the message that the soldiers were not carrying their guns and were unprepared. Many of the black people who worked with us ran away from Chitengo soon after this: our dear old Vasco led his fourteen children far away from the park and sat out the troubled time elsewhere. He is now back at Chitengo in his old job.

After that night of gunfire many more Portuguese troops were moved in to Chitengo. We later heard that our vacated house and laboratory were being used as barracks and my studio as a bar for the soldiers.

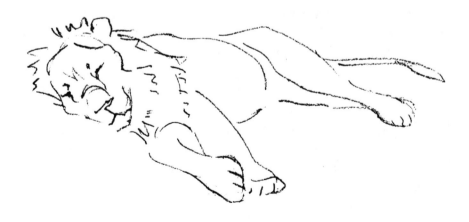

33

Moçambique's Thirstland

In October of 1973, based in Lourenço Marques and unaware of what the following six months would bring to Moçambique, we took the opportunity of spending a month in Gazaland, a very dry area some four hundred kilometres north of the capital.

Ken had already proposed that the system of seasonal floodplains, sand, and saline country called Banhine be given National Park status, and included with Moçambique's protected natural areas, as representative of the arid zone of the country. This had in fact been carried out. However, having completed an aerial survey, he realized that a ground survey must also be done and that the worst, or driest, part of the year would be the most effective time in which to do this, when the various factors controlling the plant and animal communities are strongly evident.

With both children, then aged five and three, and our simple but effective bush equipment, we headed north in the Land-Rover towards the Limpopo River and then beyond. Our first night out was spent near Inharrime, a small town on the coast which is famous for the pale aromatic indigenous coffee that is grown there. On the outskirts of this settlement is a large, slightly brackish lake that lies trapped behind the line of coastal sand dunes, and it was here that we pitched our tents well after dark. The black sky was brilliantly starred and a lone lala palm under which we camped spread pointed fingers against it. Early the next morning a veil of mist was spread out over the water before us, turning the scene into a delicate oriental print of monochrome washes and slight, etched reeds. The pale sun steadily sucked up the mist to reveal the sparkling cobalt blue expanse of the lake with a faint blue line of dunes rimming the far side. Allan and Michelle played happily in the white, fine beach sands and the glittering ripples. As the sun's heat began to

focus its full force on us we all stripped and waded out into the clear cool waters with a cake of soap and had our last good bath for three weeks. The water was like sunlit silk on our bodies and the bottom sand was firm under our feet.

We tore ourselves away from the cool brightness of the lake by mid-morning and travelled on towards the Banamana saltpan, which lies north-east of Banhine, and which we intended visiting before turning back towards our main objective. Our next overnight stop was in a shallow valley between the parallel sand ridges that cross that part of the country. An experimental dairy farm was situated in the dry thorn veld of the valley; but like so many of the Moçambique Portuguese projects the buildings looked as if they had been built in the last century and they were practically abandoned.

A winding stream coursed along between the acacias and we chose a camp site well up on the slope, away from the water and mosquitoes. On the other side of the stream were a group of *kraals* half hidden in the *miombo* woodland that extended down the sandy slope. Ken bought a chicken for five escudos from some local people and we gnawed its tough stewed flesh for our evening meal.

We rose early the next morning to pack and be on our way before the sun became too hot. From the direction of the farm a small dusty donkey appeared with a black boy slouched on its back. Allan gave a yell of delight and dashed off to beg the boy for a ride. Michelle, like her brother wearing only a pair of shorts and no shoes, ran after him on her plump little legs. Away through the short grassland and grey thorn bushes they ran, trotting at the side of the donkey until we could see them no longer. They arrived back five minutes later, scarlet-faced from the heat and exertion, sweaty and happy. The boy had given them each a ride behind him.

Michelle, who was now three, had not been out camping with us for a year and was no longer familiar with the various necessities of camp life. Sleeping in a tent or under a mosquito net was a treat, but having to squat in the open with the tall woodland trees looking down on her, or the wide plains on her back, was a different matter and one she could not get used to in a hurry. We had a special small spade with which to dig a hole and to fill it in again afterwards. But no matter how smooth the sandy patch I found for my small daughter there were always, much to her annoyance, either grass stalks or twigs or flies that would tickle her bottom.

We had left the main roads and villages, with their goats and pawpaw trees, far behind us before the bumpy sand track led on to the sunburnt flats and desiccated wooded country around Banamana pan. The area seemed devoid of people: the only *kraals* we saw were deserted and derelict, looking bomb-blasted by the furnace-like heat. Late in the afternoon we suddenly saw a lone figure amongst the palm scrub and Ken stopped to ask him if we were on the right track to the pan. He was a Shangaan and conversed with Ken in fluent Fanigolo; being well-oiled with palm beer he gave us a graphic description of his background and circumstances together with the information we required. I was struck by the withered and wrinkled appearance of the man's belly. The face was of a young man but his belly was old and shrunken, the skin in numerous folds and wrinkles. He explained that he had worked on the mines in South Africa and had returned to grow crops for his family. But at this time of the year nothing could be sown and nothing could be reaped as the heat was too intense and too dry. No rain would fall for a month or more. His people subsisted at this time on veld foods; previously they could supplement these by hunting but now—he shrugged his shoulders—game, even the springhare, was scarce. Their major food was the sap which he was at that moment tapping from a lala palm, letting

it drip into a dried calabash shell from a frond blade driven into the stem. He explained that even the babies are fed the palm sap and added poignantly that if he allowed it to ferment a little and become potent it stopped them crying from hunger.

We knew that lala palm beer is very nutritious and so had no cause to doubt that this was in fact what was keeping the people alive in this tremendously harsh environment. If it were not for boreholes put down by the Government and a few scattered trade-stores that sell meal and other less useful commodities to those few who occasionally have money, it is possible that the age-old customs of moving with the seasons to available water and to better pastures or fields would still govern these people's lifestyles and their rhythms would still be in tune with their environment rather than in discord.

The dried out saltpan, on whose white stretches we eventually arrived at five that afternoon, is thirty kilometres long by two kilometres broad. Its name, Banamana, is the Shangaan word for salt, as crusts of salt are peeled off its surface during the dry season and used or sold by the local people. *Miombo* woodland on sand, and mopane on the clayey soils, surround the pan, and as the rainfall is a meager five hundred millimetres a year the whole aspect of the place is quite unlike the lushness of most of Moçambique. In fact Banamana reminded us immediately of Etosha and the arid west of southern Africa. The pan with its mirages and white dust devils was very reminiscent of its western counterpart, the succulent purple and green salt bushes similar, and even the bird and animal life was the same as the arid zone of Namibia. Ostrich, sand grouse, violet-eared waxbill, and the typically dry-country animals, bat-eared fox and springhare, occur here. There is little game left at Banamana now, however, as it has for many years been hunted and tracked down. The sad remaining dregs of Gazaland's wildlife is to be found mostly in Banhine where surface water is more easily available.

We camped on the edge of the bleached pan surface under a small mopane which offered precious little shade but a magnificent view on three sides of us. The pup-tents pitched, and firewood collected, we built up a crackly fire of resinous mopane wood. Slowly the sun set beyond the pan, leaving a translucent green sky to darken into a glittering cool night, as refreshing and mild as the day had been thick and oppressive. The night was dark and utterly silent. No bird called, no animal stirred. The stars haloed the still branches of the mopane as we lay outside our tent with the embers of the fire at our feet and the wide wild darkness all our own.

In the morning mirages started up on the horizon only half an hour after the rise of the sun. Whilst it was still comparatively cool, the children in their pyjamas played cars over the sand ripples of the pan. At about nine o'clock I walked out alone in only hat and shoes with my sketch pad under my arm on to the white desert; the sun scorched my shoulders and blasted up on to my belly and breasts, reflecting off the bare pan. Far away baobabs and mopane shimmered in dark designs and lines. The silence was purifying, the privacy a fulfillment in itself. Sitting on a hummock of sand and I became happily absorbed in a sketch. Suddenly a quick rustling came up behind me out of the barrenness, and I leapt up in a cold sweat of fright. Imagining an animal, I saw to my relief it was a tiny dust devil, whirled up by the hot air currents, flicking dust and dry leaves and then dying away as quickly as it had started.

The heat by one or two o'clock that day was so intense that all four of us could do nothing but lie on the tarpaulin under the mopane's thin shade. Until four o'clock we were almost unable to move and the children were pale, apathetic and irritable.

We left Banamana early the next morning before the heat could build up, and ground on endlessly, jolting and bumping along the sand track that would take us to Banhine. Allan and Michelle, sitting on their comfortable platform of mattress and sleeping bags, were happier in the moving car, where there was a slight breeze coming through the open windows, and they finished off the last of our valuable supply of oranges. At last after six hours of driving through limp and lifeless woodlands we came upon a small board made of tomato box planks and on which was hand-painted the sign: *'Parque Naçional de Banhine'.*

34

The Serengeti of Moçambique

Banhine, meaning plains, is in fact an inland delta, like the Okavango swamp in Botswana. It is the meeting of a series of drainage lines or seasonal rivers that rise on the Zimbabwean border, and whose waters eventually flood through Banhine and the Shangaan drainage line into the Limpopo.

During the long dry season the delta is almost devoid of surface water, although brack water is not far below the surface. In summer the floodwaters rise and cover the plains to a greater or lesser extent. A good flood may last through to the next year, but this is unusual. More often by October ostrich once again pad over the dried out dusty stretches and large numbers of springhare graze the short green grass in the evenings.

Between the arms of the grass plains stand low sand ridges and islands. These are covered in lala palm scrub and fever trees, or a rather bizarre plant community of tall fat-jowled baobabs, purple-and-silver-skinned, and twisted green-stemmed commiphora shrubs. Under these fairy-tale-like forms grow stands of orange-spotted aloes and spiky sansivieria leaves. These little thickets are delightful, and rich in things of interest. While Ken analysed the plant communities, Allan would shimmy up the amply proportioned baobab branches like a squirrel. Michelle and I would boil up a pot of tea or hunt for snail shells and insects in the leaf litter.

We set up camp in Banhine at the site of an old hunters' safari camp. Two open huts with crumbling walls and falling thatch provided shelter for us for two weeks, far preferable to the tents which were so hot and stuffy. There being no surface water available we had brought our own supply in a forty-four-gallon petrol drum, and with great economy we managed to make do, filling it only once more before the end of our stay.

Spending the day out in the bush gathering data we would return to camp in the late afternoon. With a fire lit and a tinned food concoction heating in the pot, the children would reluctantly submit to being washed in two inches of warm water at the bottom of a basin, and then clad in pyjamas, would romp in the cool sand.

Near to our camp lived a small family of Shangaan. Each evening the father, Fabião, would come over for a chat with Ken, bringing with him a large beaker of tepid frothy palm beer. He sometimes brought his wife Rosina—a proud, powerful woman—and their pale-skinned son and daughter. The son would carry a *makweaan*—a bow-shaped musical instrument—and we would hear him strumming it to himself, the notes clear and soft.

Rosina on occasions brought me a tin of *dungula*, small red berry fruit of the shrub *Salvadora australis*. These are sweet, sticky berries and each has a single oval seed as beautifully marked as a tiny sand-grouse egg. One tinful of fruit I boiled up with sugar and strained to make a jelly jam. We ate it with fresh scones baked in the black pot and gave some to Rosina for her to try.

These berries were a boon in the bush. When the children became hot and tired we would stop at the nearest *dungula* shrub and they would busy themselves picking and eating the refreshing fruit. Allan would pick a laden branch and slowly savour the fruit for a long while after we had continued on our way. Having learnt from Ken which wild fruits are edible I am always amazed how, at almost any time of the year, we come across some fruit or other which when sucked or chewed helps immensely to refresh our energy or slake our thirst.

After camping at Banhine for a week we heard that rain had fallen to the west of us and had filled a pan lying in the mopane veld. Our drum of water was running low so we loaded it into the Rover together

with Rosina, her daughter, and a bundle of washing and drove off amidst screams of mirth and joyful singing from the two women. It was a great occasion for them to take a bath.

The pan was fairly large and around its edges was a gathering of women and children soaping clothes and filling containers, and goats quenching their thirsts.

We topped up our drum and water bottles with the slightly murky water, trying to avoid scooping up too many tadpoles and water beetles. After washing the children, I took a bucket of water into the mopane and had a simply wonderful scrub down and hair-wash with the sunlight and dappled shade playing on the warm biscuit-coloured water as it cascaded over me.

We did not come across many large animals in Banhine. This area was once called the 'Serengeti' of Moçambique because of its concentrations of game: vast herds of wildebeest and zebra used to migrate in lines across the plains and elephant and lion were abundant. But it has now been the trophy-and meat-hunters' mecca for too long and very little remains. From Fabião we heard of how a Lourenço Marques businessman had recently hired a local hunter to obtain ivory for him. The hunter had, from the safety of a tree, shot a herd of ten elephant, most of which had very small to no ivory, and had then left the carcasses lying in the bush. We saw only one herd of elephant in the two weeks we were there. There were twelve of them and they were very wary, staying bunched together far out on the plains, their dark shapes weaving and billowing in the heat haze.

The game still have a lot of room in which to move in little-developed Central Moçambique, so at this, the driest, time of the year most of what game is left in Banhine had probably migrated to better watered areas.

Only a few ostriches, some zebra and wildebeest were left and saw one beautiful male roan antelope, tawny coated and glossy.

Of the smaller animals the most conspicuous were the springhare. They are nocturnal and seldom seen in the day, but at night in the headlights of the car thousands of these rabbit-sized, kangaroo-shaped rodents would jump to and fro, their eyes reflecting the glare like the illuminations of a miniature city.

After the summer rains the flooding of the Banhine plains produces the strange phenomenon of wet-lands and wet-lands dwellers—such as waterfowl, hippo, waterbuck, and buffalo—surrounded by a harsh and arid environment. Later, the floods subside and the dry country animals spread again on to the plains—the duck, flamingo, hippo and waterbuck migrate back to the other marshes or to the Limpopo. Lung fish left behind in pools bury themselves in the mud under the dry trunks of an immense five-metre tall, pithy-stemmed water weed known locally as *mpepu*. Its scientific name is *Aeschynomene pfundi* and the soft stems are used for making floats for fishing and toys by the Shangaan children. In the dry months the people seek out slight rises in the mud that indicate lung fish nests, dig them from their slimy cavities, roast and eat them.

In a single year Banhine experiences extremes of wetness and dryness. It thus provides habitats for a spectrum of animals that depend on each. As such it is a unique area, and one prays that it may survive in these times of land plunder and strife.

35

Rabies

Our stay at Banhine was nearing its end when we noticed threateningly dark cumulo-nimbus clouds build up over the eastern horizon. A new fresh wind with a trace of moisture in it sprang up and, welcome as its coolness was, we knew that it was bringing unwelcome rain. To make sure we could get through on the rough track to the Limpopo, and then on to Lourenço Marques, we realized we would have to pack right away and leave the plains.

It was mid-afternoon when, having abandoned our camping site and given Rosina the largest of our three-legged pots as a farewell present, we drove through herds of black pigs and dull-eyed cows to the lone cattle ranch which is situated on the edge of Banhine. The ranch manager, Gonçalves, oily and dank with sweat, and in the off-white vest and khaki shorts which were the only clothes we ever saw on him, welcomed us happily. Visitors are rare and eagerly awaited on this remote ranch. We accepted his invitation to spend the night. In view of the heat and a slight sunstroke that Ken had developed the day before we did not seriously consider refusing.

Cold showers of the brack water from the borehole rejuvenated us all and the children recovered their bounce and went exploring. Vague anxieties about their treading on snakes or rusty farm implements entered my mind, but since we had spent weeks in the wildest possible surroundings with no harm befalling them, I put these thoughts aside. The shade and coolness of dusk gradually enveloped the veranda where we sat sipping incredibly satisfying iced beers in cool glasses. The children had come in and I relaxed into a blissful and satisfied semi-coma. Dogs began barking and snapping nearby and I hardly noticed them until Allan ran down the steps to investigate.

Seconds later my heart froze as the boy screamed hysterically. I found myself at the bottom of the stairs with Allan in my arms, a wet dark patch at the base of his bare back. One of the dogs had rushed up and bitten him. He sobbed, more shaken by the quickness of the attack than by the bite itself. Relieved to see that it was only a slight gash that was bleeding gently, I tried to still the fear I had felt and led Allan away to wash the wound and quiet him.

My relief however was shattered when Gonçalves questioned the servants about the brown mangy mongrel that had bitten Allan. From their replies it appeared almost certain that the dog had rabies, a disease which was apparently extremely prevalent there. It was this dog, they said, that had been running amok over the last few days, attempting to attack other dogs and people. Ken and I looked at one another, the same icy dread creeping through us both. We were over a day's drive, along excruciating tracks, from Lourenço Marques and goodness knows how long we could be delayed if it began to rain. Not knowing much about rabies, we did not know how soon a victim must be injected against it; but being near to Allan's spine the virus could possibly attack the nervous system rapidly.

I fed the children and tucked them into bed whilst the manager gave orders for his farm hands to go out with rifle and bow and arrow to hunt the dog. They did not find it, however, so we were unable to discover if it really was carrying the dreaded illness; but the odds seemed to be against us. We packed the car, laid the sleeping children in the back, and by 11 p.m. were on the track to Lourenço Marques.

It was a moonless, clouded night and Ken did not know the roads. A soft rain started to fall shortly before dawn but fortunately it did not slow our progress. For thirteen hours, without a break, we drove through the most agonizing night of my life and bleakest morning.

It was midday on Sunday when we finally and exhaustedly reached Lourenço Marques. Anyone knowing the comfort-loving Portuguese will understand that a mealtime is a bad time to get a hold of anyone, even a *medico*, and a Sunday lunchtime is that much worse. When eventually we did contact a doctor, he put our minds to rest about the delay. Only if a person is bitten on the face or head, he told us, is there any urgency about beginning the injections.

The next two weeks, during which Allan received fourteen painful injections, were a nightmare for the whole family, as the vaccine in itself can cause brain damage to a child. Fortunately he took them very successfully and with time the whole dreadful episode faded into the past.

To Ken and me it seemed significant that for three weeks we had camped in wild country, living a simple and primitive way of life close to the many dangers of the bush. But with forethought and precaution, which included a medicine kit, an antibiotic, and snake bit serum, no one had suffered any harm. No sooner however, had we set foot in a human settlement again than this horrifying incident occurred. A wild animal, with or without rabies, could have attacked Allan in the bush but the chance was very much less than at this farm, or in Lourenço Marques itself, where stray and starving dogs abound and diseases are passed around like warmth in a pot of heating water.

36

Turquoise Seas

One year's stay in Lourenço Marques brought a further opportunity for a delightful and unique trip. Ken required data on the use and abuse of coastal resorts, and on areas of Moçambique's long and beautiful coastline that were in need of protection from unplanned development. So it was arranged that we travel the south coast from Inhambane to Oro Point, the southern-most resort in Moçambique.

Pomene, a private coastal reserve and fishing resort north of Inhambane, was our starting point. We traveled there in the Land-Rover with Ken's fibre-glass surfboard as part of our equipment. This marvelous piece of coast, owned at that time by a private consortium, was completely undeveloped apart from a luxury hotel built along the lines of a Portuguese fishing village. We cleared an opening under the dune thicket, about a kilometre from the hotel, and pitched a large tent there. Ken dug a rubbish pit a little way from the camp and put up a shower shelter of reeds and branches. I thought at the time how like Ken to be so careful in his plans as to tuck our camp in the thicket, utterly protected from the wind and salt spray but at the same time completely devoid of a view. A few days later I was thankful for this seemingly unnecessary meticulousness. A cyclone suddenly blew out of the Moçambique channel and for thirty-six hours thunderous waves, ten metres high, pounded high up on to the beach, while great winds razed the vegetation exposed at its edge.

The rocky point at Pomene juts into a crystalline sapphire sea. The continental shelf is very narrow here and the sea floor plunges down to great depths not far from land. Deep-sea fish are thus found quite close to shore and Pomene is famed for its marlin and sail-fish angling. Ken, an ardent surfer, was given the fright of his life one day as the spotted shadowy form of a whale-shark, some four times the length of his board, swam slowly under him. Luckily these huge creatures are quite docile. This was not the only company he had whilst surfing at Pomene. Dolphin would sometimes ride a wave beside him, sliding down the glassy green slope whilst keeping a large bright eye on the land mammal that had invaded their element.

From the rocks the children and I used to fish and watch the big loggerhead turtles rise and dive amongst the churned white waters below us. Manta rays skimmed the waves, their upraised 'wings' cutting the water like shark dorsal fins—a terrifying sight, especially when Ken was on the water surfing.

The tidal rock pools at Pomene were particularly rich in small sea life. Brilliantly coloured coral fish and red and white banded barber-shrimps with immensely long and bristling antennae would glide gently amongst the drifting arms of anemones and seaweeds. Ken found a long thin green crab empathetic in form and colour with the ribbon-like sea-grass in which it lived. A rare goby had the same habitat and a similar elongated green camouflage. The sea-grass, a flowering plant, unlike the more primitive seaweed that reproduces by spores, forms the basic diet of the dugong, a marine mammal which occurs on the East African coast down to Lourenço Marques. Ken had at an earlier stage done an aerial survey of dugong in order to obtain some idea of their numbers and distribution. I unfortunately never got to see this ugly sausage-shaped animal which ironically enough gave rise to the myth of the mermaid. Female dugong—like elephant, strangely enough—have rounded human-like 'breasts'.

Our camp had the silvery curve of the beach in front if it and an estuary of mangroves behind it. Mangrove is the general name given to various species of trees that are especially adapted to grow in the rising and falling shallows of tidal flats. They have roots that grow upward instead of downward, protruding out of the mud in order to absorb oxygen from the air whilst the nutritious clayey silt in which the trees grow is waterlogged and stagnant. A bizarre and imaginative variety of roots occurs on the different species. Some have spongy pencil-roots that rise out of the ground in a miniature forest of spikes. Others have knee-roots, knobbled and bent, that protrude above the high-water mark. Yet

others have buttress-roots that flange out from the trunk, or long, fine roots growing down from the branches.

Mangrove swamps are very rich in aquatic life. The most conspicuous animal in the Pomene swamps was the fiddler crab, which has one huge red clipper and one small pale one. The male beckons to females, threatens rivals, and blocks his burrow entrance against invasion with the brightly coloured clipper. Mud-skippers are common in the shallows and on exposed mudbanks. Startling little fish with bulging eyes on top of their heads (like crocodile, hippo, and frogs, for peeping over the surface of the water), mud-skippers have leg-like pectoral fins upon which they clamber out of the water and climb on to mudbanks and fallen trees. They can remain out of the water for some time, provided their gills stay moist, and can move quickly overland by means of powerful flicks of the tail.

We spent hours exploring the shallow, dark and mysterious channels of the swamp, wading in the warm water, and sometimes mud, up to our knees. Ken found three mangrove tree species that were new to him as they do not occur further south along the South African coast.

Mangrove snails abound on the tree trunks and are collected and eaten by the local people. Small mangrove oysters cling to the trunks and roots too, their shells raised into bonnet-like peaks which shade them from the sun during the hours of low ebb. Shoals of prawns occur in the warm shallows and we saw a group of men with nets catch enough in half an hour to fill two large sacks.

We brought some of these prawns back to camp and grilled them to pink perfection over the fire. Seafood was readily available at Pomene; young boys would come around with buckets of big dark crab or white cockles. They sometimes brought small tomatoes, pawpaws and mangoes and tins of the sticky yellow dates from the wild Phoenix palm. During the entire coastal trip coconuts played an important part in our diet. We would buy green nuts, from which the cool juice could be drunk and the soft pulp eaten with a spoon, and ripe ones for the hard, chewy, white flesh which can be kept for several days.

From Pomene our Land-Rover ground its way along dozens of the deep sandy tracks that link the main north-south highway to little visited and remote resorts. Jangamu, a particularly delightful 'undiscovered' bay, was one such resort. Its access track was longer than most, running up and down sand rises and through the sparse grasslands and scrub of the coastal vegetation. No human habitations were to be seen at all until we reached coconut plantations strung out behind the beach dunes. We bought a bunch of nuts from one of the few black people who were evident amongst the scattered palm-frond huts.

At last we came in sight of the sea. On this turquoise coast, the water at Jangamu is bluer, the surf whiter and the smooth crescent beach more brilliant than any other. A grove of coconut palms stood on a bluff overlooking the bay; the slender, elegant trees tossed their shaggy heads and sang in the wind. An abandoned hut stood some little way away staring vacantly from under its brow of palm thatch over the bright gem-like bay and beach.

One of our last stops was at the Maputo Elephant Reserve, some sixty kilometres south of Lourenço Marques. Maputo is a large tract of land next to the sea occupying an old filled-in estuary and running back into dune ridges between which are scattered fresh-water lakes.

We spent a day on the beach of Maputo at a point with the musical name of Millibangalala. Rare, spiny palm-like cycads grow close to the beach here and the long lonely coast is visited by nesting turtles. Behind the beach low-lying plains alternate with forest-covered ridges. Up to two hundred elephant, often confettied with white egret, graze the coarse grass of these plains. I once flew over Maputo in a helicopter with Paul Dutton, an old friend and colleague of Ken's from the Moçambique Game Department. He was testing the surface water of Maputo for salinity, which decreased from north to south and determines to a certain extent the movement of the elephant in different seasons. The helicopter landed like a lost dragonfly in a sea of grass first at one waterhole and then the next. From the air the herds of elephant looked like ticks below us. They were worried, milling around with flapping ears and testing the wind with teapot-spout trunks.

The Maputo plains, marshy and green in summer, copper in winter, have a prehistoric air about them. Perhaps it is the lush coarseness of the long grass or the waving fronds of Phoenix palm that look so much like giant ferns or cycads from an age past. Perhaps it is the huge quiet forms of the elephant feeding in groups over the flat grasslands and disappearing into specks in the coastal haze of the distance.

From Maputo we drove along the packed damp sands of the beach until finally we reached Oro Point, our last port of call. From there we reluctantly made our way back along the roads to Lourenço Marques.

Some few months after our coastal trip we packed our household goods and moved from Moçambique to Pretoria, South Africa, where Ken was to begin work on his doctoral thesis. Three weeks after we left Lourenço Marques the revolution in Portugal occurred and the subsequent events resulted in the old colony of Moçambique being handed over to the new regime under the Frelimo movement.

Once the new government has recovered from its teething pains we hope that Ken's plan for Gorongosa will be implemented. In the meantime the wild stretches of country of Moçambique remain very much a part of us—and will survive as we knew them in our writings and drawings, if not in reality. Continual change *is* life and nothing can ever be held as it was, but it can be recorded, and this we hope to continue to do. Other lonely beaches and wild living landscapes lie ahead of us, holding mysteries and meanings, patterns and cycles as old as the earth itself and still, as yet, incompletely understood.

Printed in the United States
146596LV00002BA/1/P